T5-CQA-939

The Purpose
of
A Christian School

David B. Cummings, editor

Presbyterian and Reformed Publishing Company
Phillipsburg, New Jersey 08865

Copyright 1979

CHRISTIAN EDUCATION ASSOCIATION

ISBN: 0-87552-157-6

Printed in the United States of America

Contents

INTRODUCTION

The tomatoes on a garden plant that have been uprooted by a storm soon rot and die. Likewise, where there are no roots in Jesus Christ, there are no good fruits. This is why we live in a society where the rotten fruits of ungodliness are increasingly apparent.

John Dewey, whose writings have become the "bible" of modern education, has proposed false roots which have only quickened the pace of rotting in our age. He says that "to set up any end outside of education, as furnishing its goal and standard, is to deprive the educational process of much of its meaning and tends to make us rely upon false and external stimuli in dealing with the child." We must "let the child's nature fulfill its own destiny." The glory of God is ruled out as the purpose, or end, of education. God's Word is ruled out as a standard of truth and righteousness. Such considerations are, for modern government-controlled education, mere "false and external" stimuli which interfere with the pupil's advancement up the ladder of human progress.

Where can I get biblical guidance for training my children that is understandable?

In the face of such man-centeredness, the present volume

takes a vigorous stand with biblical Christianity against those who have cut themselves off from their roots; the present volume heralds a return to man's root-relationship with the living God. Like a plant cut off from its roots, apart from Christ we can do nothing. In union with him by faith, the lives of PARENTS, PUPILS, and TEACHERS bear bountiful fruits of righteousness in the midst of the world to the glory of God. This is the God-given purpose of Christian schools, and thus the outline of this volume. With J. Gresham Machen we believe in Christian schools for the sake of preserving Christianity and God-centered living on the face of the earth. It was the burden of communicating this in an understandable and convincing way to the evangelical community that led a group of individuals to form the Christian Education Association "to assist Christian educators and concerned parents in the task of teaching their children through the collection, publication, and distribution of literature produced by competent Christian writers." In chapter 1 Calvin Cummings succinctly urges the importance of Christian schools as an arm of the home; the school is to supplement the parents' instruction of their children without usurping the family as the basic unit for Christian education of the young. He touches upon some specific areas (e.g., discipline and sex education) where parents should be vitally concerned that the school support and not negate the Christian instruction given in the home.

In chapter 2 John Sanderson does not opt for a Christian school which produces academically inferior pupils. Nor does he support the ideal of head-stuffed hypocrites. Drawing from the example of Timothy he unfolds realistic ways that pupils might be encouraged to enthusiastically give their lives to service in the church and in the world. Consideration is given to the implications that such practical application of knowledge might have upon the curriculum.

Noel Weeks, in chapter 3, offers teachers (and all concerned about the relation of our Christian faith to the rest of our life) basic principles for using the Bible in the classroom, whether the class be math, history, literature, or botanical classification! The question is not, Is the Bible relevant?, but *how* should I use it. Here is concrete help.

The fourth chapter by Leonard Coppes addresses a general question for parent, pupil, and teacher--how much is a Christian school education really worth? There are financial sacrifices. There are sacrifices of prestige. Having a Christian school takes the involvement of many who will commit much time. In this chapter we are directed onward in our endeavors with eyes outward on the world we wish to influence, rather than with eyes directed inward to meditate on our own martyrdom.

Finally, Cornelius Van Til ties together the Christ-centered theme which pervades the volume. The goal of a Christian school is no less than the goal of all of life. The goal of our child's schooling must be the same as the rest of his life--that he offer himself as a living sacrifice "seeking to do everything to God's glory." Not the man-centeredness of Dewey but the God-centeredness of the Bible must dominate the classroom!

To insure that this volume and subsequent volumes reach our goals, the Christian Education Association has enlisted the help of associate editors to read and evaluate manuscripts as to their academic quality and their ability to communicate understandably to a general audience. We are grateful to Dr. John Skilton, Dr. Robert Ream, Rev. Ronald Nickerson, and Professor Raymond Zorn for their contributions to this volume as associate editors. Thanks to Mr. Craig and Presbyterian and Reformed Publishing Company for their support and encouragement. I would also personally thank each member of the Christian Education Association for the time they have given to the corresponding, editing, and typing which has preceded and followed the work done by the associate editors. Special thanks to Mr. William Haden, Jr., Mr. and Mrs. Douglas Felch, and Mr. Daryl Docktor, who from the initial stages shared the labors for a vision which has now become a reality in the Lord.

David B. Cummings, M. Div.
Editor

Chapter 1
PARENTS
The Purpose of a Christian School Is . . .

*That the Christian Parents Might Be Helped to Fulfill
Their Responsibility to God for Their Children*

CALVIN K. CUMMINGS*

The first basic purpose of the Christian school is to help Christian parents fulfill their responsibility to God for their children.

There are three institutions that God has established on earth for man's good and God's glory. They are: the church, the state, and the family. In the Bible, God prescribes the function of each of these institutions.

Christ established the church as a divine institution when he declared that upon the apostle's confession, "Thou art the Christ, the Son of the living God," he would build his church (Matt. 16:18). Christ and his apostles define for us the spiritual tasks of the church. The church is to teach and preach the Word for the edifying of believers and their children (John 17:15-17; Acts 20:28) and for the evangelizing of the lost (Matt. 28:19-20). It is the church's task to administer the

---

*Rev. Calvin K. Cummings, M.Div., is the founder of Trinity Christian School, Pittsburgh, Pa. He has served as a pastor in the Orthodox Presbyterian Church for 40 years. He was an active leader in the movement which saw legislation passed to provide free busing for Christian school pupils in Pennsylvania.

sacraments of Baptism and the Lord's Supper (Matt. 28:19; I Cor. 11:23-29). To the church is committed the responsibility of exercising discipline among its members (Matt. 16:19; 18:17; I Cor. 5:1, 4-5). Nowhere does Christ commit to the church the responsibility of teaching such subjects as reading, writing, and arithmetic, or the arts and sciences.

God has also established the state as a divine institution. We read in the Scriptures: "Let every soul be subject unto the higher powers. For there is no power but of God, the powers that be are ordained of God" (Romans 13:1). The function of the state as prescribed in Scripture is to administer justice and mercy in man's relation to his fellow man. The state is to be "the minister of God for good; the ruler "beareth not the sword in vain" (Rom. 13:4). There is no authority in Scripture for the state's taking over the responsibility for the education of children from Christian homes. To do so is a usurpation of the authority over children which belongs to the Christian family. This brings us to a consideration of the function of the family, in particular the Christian family, in the education of children.

The Lord established the family as a divine institution when he created a helper suitable for man and instructed them to "be fruitful and multiply" (Gen. 1:28; 2:18). The family is the most basic unit of society. The state and the church will be what its families are. The fifth commandment, "Honor thy father and thy mother," is the divine law that is to govern all families. Children are to respect and obey their parents. This presupposes that parents are to exercise authority over their children. Parents are primarily responsible for teaching children what is right and wrong and then seeing that they obey.

God in his Word makes it clear to Christian parents that they, primarily, are responsible for the education of their children. In Old Testament times he commanded parents: "And these words, which I command thee this day, shall be in thine heart: and thou shalt teach them diligently unto thy children, and shalt talk of them when thou sittest in thine house, and when thou walkest by the way, and when thou liest down and when thou risest up" (Deut. 6:6-7). "My son, hear the instruction of thy father, and forsake not the law of thy mother" (Prov. 1:8) was Solomon's admonition to youth. "Train up a child in the way he should go: and when he is old, he will not depart from it" (Prov. 22:6) was Solomon's instruction to parents. In New Testament times the responsibility for the Christian education of children was placed squarely on the shoulders of the fathers. "And, fathers, do not provoke your children to anger; but bring them up in the discipline and instruction of the Lord" (Eph. 6:4).

It is the responsibility of Christian parents to seek to provide a God-centered and Christ-honoring education for their children. "The fear of the Lord is the beginning of wisdom: and the knowledge of the holy is understanding" (Prov. 9:10). "Casting down imaginations, and every high thing that exalteth itself against the knowledge of God, and bringing into captivity every thought to the obedience of Christ" (II Cor. 10:5). Of Christ we read that "all things were created by him, and for him . . . and by him all things consist . . . that in all things he might have the preeminence" (Col. 1:16-18).

Today Christian parents face a most formidable obstacle as they seek to fulfill their responsibility of providing a Christian education for their children. That obstacle is the public educational system maintained by public taxation. In the eighteenth and early nineteenth centuries most of the schools which provided for the education of the public were Christian schools. The local school boards were predominantly Christian. The Bible was an integral part of the child's education. The McGuffy Readers (1836-57) were used extensively in public schools. These readers abounded in Christian teaching such as "In Adam's fall we sinned all." In 1835, however, a step was taken that was to end in the elimination of God, the Bible, and Christ from all public schools in the nation.

3

Horace Mann, a noted educator in New England, sold the country on the Prussian system of education by State taxation. At this juncture the State took over the education of youth and there began the process of eliminating Christian teaching from the classroom. By the authority of the Supreme Court, Bible reading and prayer are now forbidden in the classroom. The public school system has become completely godless in its instruction except for the phrase "under God" in the pledge to the flag.

The completely secular character of the modern public school confronts the Christian parent with a most solemn responsibility. Christian parents should realize that during the most impressionable years of their children's lives and for five hours each school day they are being trained in the public schools to think, believe, and live apart from God. They should recognize the fact that they are consenting to have their children taught this way and that as parents they are responsible for the effects of such teaching on their thoughts and lives.

How can Christian parents best fulfill their God-given responsibility to provide a God-centered, Christ-honoring education? They can join hands with other Christian parents to provide a truly Christian education. Most parents will find that they are not in a position to teach their children at home. Father works away from home and mother frequently lacks adequate time to teach effectively. More basically, few parents are qualified to teach all the subjects for all ages. But these Christian parents can band together to secure the services of trained and dedicated Christian teachers to teach their children. Then you have a Christian school. It is the purpose of the Christian school to assist Christian parents who desire a Christian education for their children.

The Christian school, basically, is an extension of the home. A Christian school should be a parent-controlled school. Christian parents are to determine the character of the teachings to be imparted to their children. An association (or society) of Christian parents and supporters determines the

4

character of the education to be provided for the children. The association of parents selects the Board of Directors to secure teachers and provide a curriculum consonant with the Christian commitment of the parents.

With this biblical concept of a Christian school, it becomes apparent what the relation of the teacher is to be to the parent and the child, and what the child's attitude is to be toward the teacher. The teacher is to be regarded as standing in the place of the parent. This means that to the best of his ability he is to seek to provide an education in agreement with the desires of the parents as expressed in the constitution of the association. It means that the teacher is to exercise the authority in the classroom that a parent would. For the child, it means that parents are to teach their children to respect and obey their teachers as they respect and obey their parents. This view of the parent-teacher-pupil relationship is essential to the learning process in the classroom. Without it there will be the breakdown of discipline in the classroom, which is working havoc in so many schools today.

Christian parents need to be aware that there are some today who, in the name of Christian education, hold that the teacher is sovereign in the classroom and operates independently of the parents. In *To Prod the Slumbering Giant,* H. Van Riessen has written, "Parents have authority over their children within the family; they do not have authority over the school." In the same book, A. Peetom states that "the staff 'runs' the school." This view torpedoes the whole biblical concept of the Christian parent. The teacher may stand against the Christian parent in his view of the Bible and the philosophy of education and the parent can say or do nothing about it. This is a usurpation of the authority that scripturally belongs to parents.

Parents who have children in a Christian school will need to guard against the danger of letting the Christian school become a substitute for the Christian home. The Christian school is to supplement the teaching and training of the home and is not to take the place of home teaching and

5

training. The Christian family is the basic unit God has provided for the Christian education of our young. Children need the instruction and example by parents in the home as a foundation on which the school and church may build.

That Christian Parents Might Be Helped to Train Their Children to Be Christ-like

The second basic purpose of the Christian school is to assist Christian parents in their God-given task of bringing up their children to be Christ-like.

The end of all Christian instruction is that "we all come in the unity of the faith, and of the knowledge of the Son of God, unto a perfect man, unto the measure of the stature of the fullness of Christ: That we henceforth be no more children, tossed to and fro, and carried about with every wind of doctrine, by the sleight of men, and cunning craftiness, whereby they lie in wait to deceive. But speaking truth in love, may grow up into him in all things, which is the head, even Christ" (Eph. 4:13-15). While, in the context, this is the goal of the teaching of the church, it is evident that it is to be the goal of the teaching of the Christian family as well. The church and the Christian school concentrate on different aspects of Christian education, but their goals are one--that we "may grow up into him in all things," that we may mature into Christ-likeness.

How does the Christian school assist the family and the church in achieving this glorious goal?

There are certain misconceptions in the minds of some Christian parents and educators concerning the way the Christian school helps parents rear children to be more Christ-like.

There are Christian parents and educators who hold that the Christian school helps parents by providing a racially segregated education. Reputedly, this makes available a better education academically and culturally. Experiences in

6

racially integrated Christian schools prove otherwise. Regardless of the pros and cons on this issue, to deny admittance of children from a Christian family on the basis of the pigment of their skin is not Christ-like. It teaches parents and children to be not like Christ. In Christ "there is neither Jew nor Greek . . . ; all are one in Christ" (Gal. 3:28). How can we teach our children to be Christ-like by being so unlike Christ? What a shame to the name of Christ to have such schools go by the name of Christian. It was a sad day when a court in our land had to declare that the racial discrimination of a Christian school was an act depriving a citizen of his constitutional right.

Other Christian parents have come to regard the Christian school primarily as a means of isolating or shielding their children from the growing immorality of the youth attending public schools. Now it is the responsibility of the Christian school to provide a wholesome Christian atmosphere both morally and spiritually. This is something to be desired. But this is not the great purpose of the Christian school--to segregate youth from the world. In fact, children from Christian homes are still sinners and some of them the worst of sinners. What is more, our Lord prayed "not that thou shouldest take them out of the world, but that thou shouldest keep them from the evil" (John 17:15). We cannot garrison our children against sin by isolation from sinners. The only sure garrison against sin is a heart renewed and sanctified by the Spirit of God.

Nor is it the chief purpose of the Christian school to help parents by providing simply a better education. Increasingly, parents are recognizing that academically many public schools are deteriorating and Christian schools frequently provide a superior education. Rightly, it should be the aim of every Christian school to excel academically. It is part of our Christian commitment to do all things to the glory of God. This requires that we seek to excel in every area of academic endeavor. The Christian teacher is to seek to excel both in

7

the content and method of his teaching. The pupil is to be motivated to learn to the full capacity of his ability. Academic achievement, however, is not the greatest contribution that the Christian school makes to the Christian family. There is a much greater contribution the Christian school makes in the teaching of the child.

The greatest contribution that the Christian school makes to the education of the child is the teaching of a Christian world-and-life view. It is the integration of Christian truth in all areas of learning. The Christian school teacher helps the children to become Christ-like by communicating to them the mind of Christ. They are taught to bring every thought into captivity to the obedience of Christ, to think Christ's thoughts after him. The light of Christ's word is shed upon the study of Christ's world.

The Christian world-and-life view is imparted first by seeing all things through the eyes of Christ; in the laws of mathematics to see the wisdom of God in Christ that established these laws; in the study of nature to see revealed the wisdom, power, and goodness of God; in history to see the unfolding of God's purposes in the world. "For of him, and through him, and to him are all things" (Rom. 11:36).

After the child is taught to see all things through the eyes of Christ, he is then taught to do all things to the honor of Christ and the glory of God. "For ye are bought with a price: therefore glorify God in your body, and in your spirit, which are God's" (I Cor. 6:20). "Whether therefore ye eat, or drink, or whatsoever ye do, do all to the glory of God" (I Cor. 10:31). In every area of human endeavor, the Christian is to seek, reclaim and restore a creation marred and a humanity ruined by the fall. This is to be done in order that something of the original God-created excellence may again be seen in the work of his hands, and that men may truly reflect the character of their creator (Ps. 19:1; Eph. 4:24).

The glorious aim of Christian school education is summed up in the words of George Herbert:

A man that looks on glasse
On it may stay his eye,
Or, if he pleaseth, through it passe,
And then the heavens espie
Teach me, my God and King,
In all things thee to see,
And what I do in anything
To do it as for thee.

What a tremendous blessing such an education is in the thought and life of the child. Intellectually, life becomes meaningful and purposeful. In Christ "all things hold together" (Col. 1:17). With the Christian view of the world, life makes sense. In Christ we have the answer to life's basic questions: Where did I come from? Why am I here? and Where am I going? These are profound questions of deep concern to all. These questions, man in his wisdom cannot answer. Only Christ in his Word has the answers.

A Christian school is a great blessing morally to the child. Children need to be told what is right and wrong and then need to be required to do the right. They do not know what is right and wrong, and when they are told, they don't by nature do the right. In the Christian school there is an authoritative standard of right and wrong--the moral law. The moral law is taught and applied in every area of human behavior. The teacher is delegated the authority by God to exercise discipline in the classroom. This brings to the child a sense of security and to the classroom an atmosphere conducive to learning. In the classroom the Christian teacher deals with the child in the same manner that the Christian parent does in the home. Thereby the child is further undergirded and fortified morally for life.

A Christ-centered education is a rich blessing spiritually. Just to live in the presence of a Christian teacher who walks with God and reflects Christ in words and works is a benediction in the life of a child. Children are deeply influenced by the life of the Christian teacher. They may soon forget the things taught, but for a long time the sweet influence of a life lived as in the presence of God will linger. The teacher's loving concern for the child, the kind words of encouragement, and the firm acts of discipline are means that the Holy Spirit uses to help form Christ in the child's heart. If our children received no other benefit than this from the Christian school, this blessing alone would be worth any sacrifice involved in sending our children to a Christian school.

Christian parents must be aware that most of the teaching in the lower and higher levels of education in America is in sharp and total conflict with the Christian parents' desire that their children have the mind of Christ.

Almost a hundred years ago Dr. A. A. Hodge of Princeton Seminary wrote:

> If every party in the state has the right of excluding from public schools whatever he does not believe to be true, then he that believes most must give way to him that believes least, and he that believes least must give way to him that believes absolutely nothing, no matter in how small a minority the atheists and agnostics may be.

> I am as sure as I am of the fact of Christ's reign that a comprehensive and centralized system of national education, separated from religion, as is now commonly proposed, will prove the most appalling enginery for the propagation of anti-Christian and atheistic unbelief and of anti-social nihilistic ethics, social and political, which this sin-rent world has ever seen.

We see the shocking fulfillment of this prophecy before our very eyes today. Let us take a good honest look at what is taking place in public schools today.

Secular humanism is the underlying philosophy of the public school educational system. It is secular as opposed to sacred, since God has no place in the instruction. It is humanistic in that man is at once the source and end of all knowledge. Man's mind is the criterion of all truth. Man's improvement is the end of all learning. This is the precise opposite of Christianity, which affirms that God is the source of all truth and his glory the end of all learning. John Dewey, whose philosphy still dominates public school education, has written: "We affirm that genuine values and tenable ends and ideals are to be derived from what is found within the movement of experience. Hence, we deny that they can be derived from authority, human or supernatural, or from any transcendent source" (*The Underlying Philosophy of Education,* p. 252). Charles Silberman in his widely read book *Crisis in the Classroom* proceeds on this same basic philosophy. An education without God can only undermine faith in God. Human experience is made the key to knowledge. There is no absolute standard of truth and error, or right or wrong. What is true and right today may be untrue or wrong tomorrow. Everything is relative, not absolute. The unproven theory of evolution is taught as fact in contradiction to the Christian doctrine of creation.

Because of the growing number of broken homes and the increasing permissiveness of parents, the problem of discipline in public schools has become crucial. Listen to Dr. James Dobson, an Assistant Professor of Pediatrics and a Director of Behavioral Research and Child Development in California, as he describes the problem of classroom discipline:

It has been estimated that 80 percent of the teachers who quit their jobs after the first year do so because of an inability to maintain discipline in their classroom.

Despite the will of the majority, the anti-disciplinarians have had their way. The rules governing student conduct have been cut down, and in their place have come a myriad of restrictions on educators. Educators find it very

11

difficult to punish or expel a student. Teachers are so conscious of parental militancy that they often withdraw from the defiant challenges of their students. As a result, academic discipline lies at the point of death in the nation's schools (*Dare to Discipline*, pp. 94, 98).

The teacher's authority in the classroom is being seriously undermined. Without recognition and exercise of that authority, there can be no effective classroom control. Without this control children cannot learn properly. It is only when parents, teachers, and pupils together recognize and submit to God's authority in conduct that effective discipline can be exercised.

The sex education programs being introduced in many public schools provide instruction in this important realm that is altogether contrary to the Christian ethic at vital points. We may expect that more and more children will be exposed to these programs.

SIECUS (Sex Information and Education Council of the United States) provides programs of sex education from kindergarten to college. Many school districts are availing themselves of these programs.

What is the basic morality of SIECUS? Let the SIECUS personnel and publications speak for themselves: "It is not the job of any voluntary health organization, which SIECUS is, to make moral judgements; SIECUS can be neither for nor against illegitimacy, premarital sex—nor any other manifestation of human sexual phenomena" (*SIECUS BROCHURE*, 1967-8, p. 5). "The choice of a premarital sexual standard is a personal moral choice, and no amount of facts or trends can 'prove' scientifically that one ought to choose a particular standard. Thus, the individual is in a sense 'free' " (*SIECUS STUDY GUIDE*, No. 5, p. 15). The Executive Director of SIECUS, Dr. Mary Calderone, in response to the question, "What is your opinion of premarital sex relations among teenagers?" replied: "What's yours? Nobody from on high

12

determines this. You determine it, . . . I don't believe . . . the old 'thou shalt nots' apply anymore" (See *Look Magazine*, March 8, 1966).

There you have it--sex education without God and his standard of morality. Moral relativism and "situation ethics" have supplanted God's standard of morality rooted in his holiness and love. Teaching sex apart from God's view of sex can only lead to a perversion of sex and sink our youth into a morass of immorality. Then America may well become another Sweden, notorious for its sexual license.

Probably the most dangerous innovation in public education today is the practice of Transcendental Meditation.

Transcendental Meditation (TM) has already achieved a semi-established status in Illinois. The State House of Representatives on May 24, 1972, passed a resolution, HR677, providing among other things "that all educational institutions, especially those under State of Illinois jurisdiction, be strongly encouraged to study the feasibility of courses in Transcendental Meditation and the Science of Creative Intelligence on their campuses and in their facilities. . . ." A similar resolution, ACR 66, has been introduced into the California State Assembly by Oakland assemblyman Ken Meade. But it remained for the federal government to be the first to appropriate funds for the spread of Transcendental Meditation; a National Institute of Health grant provided $21,540 for training 130 high school teachers as instructors in the Science of Creative Intelligence (SCI) at Humboldt State College, California, during August, 1972. (SCI is the doctrinal and TM the practical aspect of the system of yoga taught by the Maharishi.) As a result of this federal generosity, TM is being taught in high schools in a considerable number of states not previously reached.

In Pittsburgh, Transcendental Meditation was outlined for district teachers at Carnegie-Mellon University in May, 1974.

It is held that Transcendental Meditation is a science, not a religion. However, the founder and head of the movement,

Maharishi Mahesh Yogi, in his writings, makes it clear that the Transcendental Meditation advocated is religious--a variant of Hinduism.

TM as taught by Maharishi Mahesh Yogi really is a form of yoga. In an article "Meditation is Metatherapy"appearing in the *Journal of Transpersonal Psychology* (vol. 3, no. 1, 1971), Daniel Goleman from Harvard said: "TM, like most yoga systems taught in the United States, traces its roots back to the tradition of which Patanyali's Yoga Sutras is the classic statement. Now 'yoga' is a Sanskrit word for 'union,' and the final object of yoga is union with God. A yogi such as the Maharishi is one who is supposed to have attained union with God or 'God-consciousness.' " In *Meditation of the Maharishi Mahesh Yogi*, the Maharishi says, "Transcendental Meditation is a path to God" (p. 59). In reply to a direct question recorded in the same book, "Is this meditation prayer?," the Maharishi answers, "A very good form of prayer is this meditation which leads us to the field of the Creator, to the source of Creation, to the field of God" (p. 95). In the *Science of Being and Art of Living*, for example, the Maharishi writes, "The key to the fulfillment of every religion is found in the regular practice of transcendental deep meditation" (p. 264).

Can Christian parents expect that Christ will be formed in their children by a meditation which seeks to attain unto union with God without Christ? Jesus said, "I am the way, the truth, and the life: no man cometh unto the Father, but by me" (John 14:6).

We can only conclude that just as truly as a Christ-centered education helps the Christian parent in the training of the child to become like Christ in thought and life, so education without God and Christ can only serve to hinder Christian parents in their desire to have their children think and live like Christ.

Chapter 2
PUPIL
The Purpose of a Christian School Is . . .

That the Pupil Might Serve the Lord
JOHN SANDERSON, JR.*

When God sets out to do something, or commands us to do it, you can be sure that certain basic things will already have happened: first, he will have given us clear teachings about it in the Bible; second, he will provide all that is required to do it well; third, he will show us by examples how to do it, and by those examples encourage us to believe that it is possible.

In this chapter, where we are looking at one of the goals of Christian education, it will be well to look first at an example, then at the instruction, and finally at the provision given by God.

*Dr. John W. Sanderson, Jr. was one of the founders, and for five years a board member of the Wilmington Christian School. He also served as a board member, and president of the board of the Willow Grove Christian School. Recently Dr. Sanderson has left his teaching position at Covenant College in order to take up duties at Covenant Seminary, St. Louis. As members of the Reformed Presbyterian Synod, Rev. and Mrs. Sanderson have been Christian School society members and contributors in the various places they have resided. His publications include *The Fruit of the Spirit* and *Encounter in the Non-Christian Era.*

The Example of Timothy

1. Timothy, the Pupil with Genuine Concern for Others

Although he did not go to a Christian school in any modern sense of the word, Timothy is a good example of what a student of a Christian school should become. Of him, Paul wrote: "I have no one like him, who takes a genuine interest in your welfare. For everyone looks out for his own interests, not those of Jesus Christ. But you know that Timothy has proved himself, because as a son with his father he has served with me in the work of the gospel" (Phil. 2:20-22, NIV).

Paul was in prison, and yet he continued to have a concern for his Christian friends in Philippi. He wanted a report on their progress and so looked for a person who could be trusted to have a helpful ministry among the Philippians, assess their true spiritual state, and then bring back a report. It is an interesting commentary on the church of the first century that of all the men around Paul at this time, only one of them was not disqualified in Paul's eyes. Only Timothy could possibly fulfill the mission Paul had for him.

Paul prepared the way for Timothy by telling the Philippians about him. He would have a *genuine concern for them.* The opposite of 'genuine' is 'phony' or 'hypocritical.' Probably there were others who would put on a show of concern, "a bedside manner," but their real interest would be in something else. They would give a glowing report of the number of calls they made; or be more interested in making a study of the Philippians and their growth as a church. In any case, they would not be interested in the Philippians as people.

Perhaps Timothy was motivated to this concern by the example of Epaphroditus, whom Paul mentions in this same chapter (cf. v. 25). Epaphroditus had risked his life to bring a gift of money from the Philippians to Paul. He had fallen sick and almost died. But during that illness his greatest concern was that the Philippians might hear of it and might become overly concerned for him. Quite a contrast between Epaph-

16

roditus and some others who when they are ill feel that their friends are not concerned enough about them! Even when he was at the point of death, this godly pastor's thoughts were on the spiritual state of others.

Where do people like Timothy and Epaphroditus get this interest in others? Of course, it comes from an understanding of the gospel, and the gospel should always be taught so that this personal element is seen. Paul tells us that the Father chose us in Christ before the foundation of the world. He chose us not indiscriminately, but as persons. He knew us by name; our names were written on the palms of his hands. It is true that God is the high lofty one who inhabits eternity; it is also true that he dwells "with the contrite and lowly of spirit" (Isa. 57:15).

Not only so, but the Son died for us on the cross: he died for us not indiscriminately, but as persons. Paul could say, "He loved *me*, and gave himself for *me*" (Gal. 2:20). At the heart of the gospel is not only God's choice, but also the substitutionary atonement: "All of us like sheep have gone astray, each of us has turned to his own way; but the Lord has caused the iniquity of us all to fall on Him" (Isa. 53:6).

This concern for others, evident in the Father's choosing and in the Son's dying, is seen again and again in the life and teaching of our Lord on earth. Matthew, as he watched Jesus teach and heal, was impressed by his gentleness and compassion, and recalled Isaiah's prophecy, "A bruised reed he will not break, and a smoldering wick he will not quench" (cf. Matt. 12:20, NIV). It may well be that Timothy was in on many of the conversations between Paul and Luke as the latter reported on what he had learned of Christ's life and ministry.

For thirty years now I have been teaching graduates of Christian schools on both the college and the seminary level. And how many of them were Timothys? Not many; not as many as I would have expected. They knew the doctrines, but frequently the doctrines were points to be disputed and defended rather than motivations that elicited concern for

17

others. It is just here that a Christian school must make its stress. Each pupil must be shown God's concern for people so that the same concern will be engendered in them.

One of the most exciting verses in the New Testament is Galatians 4:19, "My children, with whom I am again in labor until Christ is formed in you."—"Until Christ is formed in you!" Christian education is a labor of love which is incomplete until the pupil begins to show the Savior's character trait of genuine concern for others.

2. Timothy, the Pupil Who Seeks Christ's Interests

In Philippians 2, we should also note that Paul mentions a second characteristic of Timothy which would stand him in good stead during his stay in Philippi, namely, *seeking the interests of Jesus Christ* (v. 21). Here we find the key to Timothy's compassion and genuineness in his horizontal relationships. In contrast to others who were with Paul at this time, Timothy had placed the interests of Jesus Christ at the top of his list of priorities. It is this vertical relationship which makes the horizontal possible. Without this, the gospel is reduced to a human ethic, a matter of outward conformity.

The truth which Timothy had mastered, or better, the truth which had mastered him, has received different names down through the years. It has been called "the Lordship of Christ," "the sovereignty of God," or "the Christ-centered life." One of the key passages which teaches this truth is the earlier part of Philippians 2: "Therefore God exalted him to the highest place and gave him the name that is above every name, that at the name of Jesus every knee should bow, in heaven and on earth and under the earth, and every tongue confess that Jesus Christ is Lord, to the glory of God the Father" (vv. 9-11, NIV). This passage is an expansion of Jesus' own words in Matthew 28: "All authority in heaven and on earth has been given to me." We should note the significance of this. In a sense Jesus had such authority from all eternity. After all, is he not God? But it is also wonderfully true that when he rose from the dead, having conquered death and sin, and the powers of darkness as well, he

18

received that messianic authority which he is to exercise until all things are put under his feet.

Now then, everyone in the world will someday recognize and confess that Jesus is sovereign. He is sovereign today even though a great many people do not confess him! Those who do not accept his rule now will be forced to recognize it later on—when it is too late. But there are some, in varying degrees, who confess him as Lord today. Every Christian does. To confess Jesus as Lord is not a second step in our pilgrim walk; it is involved in the very initial act of becoming a Christian. But not everyone realizes this, and not everyone realizes it to the extent that Timothy did. Timothy had no interests which were not also the interests of Jesus Christ!

Where did Timothy get this sense of God's sovereignty? Of course, he saw it illustrated in men like Epaphroditus and Paul. It is probably better communicated by example than by precept although the Bible is full of the teaching from cover to cover. This is why Christian school board members and teachers must be women and men of God in whose lives the students can see the grace of God at work. Timothy saw Epaphroditus "risking his life to make up for the help" which the Philippians could not give Paul. He was doubtless with Paul during some of the harrowing experiences mentioned in II Corinthians 11:23-28, "I have worked much harder, been in prison more frequently, been flogged more severely, and been exposed to death again and again. . . ."

Perhaps this is why in God's good providence many Christian schools go through one difficulty after another. They are often on the verge of financial collapse; many do not have the conveniences and equipment which would make the lives of teachers and board members happier. On the other hand, how else could the pupils see the grace of God at work? In my own experiences as a pupil, I remember the teachers who were real people long after I have forgotten what they taught and, sadly, I recall the teachers who just "had a job" and can remember the bitterness they engendered in us their students. The pupil who is to follow Timothy's example and seek Christ's interests instead of the interests of his own report card, must see that same example in his teachers, parents, and board members.

3. Timothy, the Pupil Who Is Enthusiastic About the Gospel

Timothy had a third character trait which stands as an ideal for Christian schools to pursue, for Paul could say of him that "as a son with his father he has served with me in the work of the gospel" (v. 22). I think most of us parents know how difficult it is for some children to do their chores. They complain about them; they put off doing them; they do them half-heartedly. But many fathers know the joy of seeing those same children come alive and work with diligence and even enthusiasm when they are their father's partners. I recall one instance when one of our sons was told to clean up his room, and a struggle of will ensued until he took his father by the hand and said, "Daddy, help." And what a job of cleaning he did because he was working with his father! I suspect this is what Paul has in mind. Timothy was *enthusiastic about the gospel* with the same sort of enthusiasm seen in a son who works with his father.

Other people in Paul's day knew the enthusiasm which comes from the gospel. Paul had seen it in the Thessalonians: "In spite of severe suffering, you welcomed the message with joy given by the Holy Spirit" (I Thess. 1:6). It is important to note that the enthusiasm we are talking about is not the result of a psychological gimmick; it is not induced by manipulation. It is something which comes from God himself, and that is why it triumphs over affliction, and often even accompanies it. But the enthusiasm did not drop out "of the blue"; it came when the Thessalonians heard and believed the Scriptures. "And we also thank God continually because, when you received the word of God, which you heard from us, you accepted it not as the word of men, but as it actually is, the word of God, which is at work in you who believe" (I Thess. 2:13).

20

Where do people like Timothy and the Thessalonians get this enthusiasm? Of course, they get it from the Scriptures, but they get it from the Scriptures when the teacher and preacher are enthusiastic themselves! The Bible is such an exciting book that it almost takes a gift to make it dull and uninteresting! Unfortunately, however, some who aspire to teach it seem to have that gift.

Timothy's knowledge of the Scriptures came from his very early days. Although he had a Greek father, his upbringing was according to the Jewish Scriptures: ". . . from infancy you have known the holy Scriptures which are able to make you wise for salvation through faith in Christ Jesus" (II Tim. 3:15, NIV).

When Paul arrived in Lystra on his second missionary journey, he found that Timothy and his mother Eunice were already believers. Perhaps they had been converted on the occasion of Paul's first visit there (Acts 14); certainly that would be true in Timothy's case since Paul speaks of him as "my true son in the faith (I Tim. 1:2). But Timothy's training as a child was at the knees of godly Eunice and her faithful mother Lois (cf. II Tim. 1:5). Paul mentions their faith which from the human point of view engendered Timothy's. As children of Abraham they claimed the promises of the Abrahamic covenant. After all, had not God said, "And I will establish my covenant between me and you and your descendants after you throughout their generations for an everlasting covenant, to be a God to you and to your descendants after you" (Gen. 17:7); and again, "The loving-kindness of the Lord is from everlasting to everlasting on those who fear him, and his righteousness to children's children, to those who keep his covenant, and remember his precepts to do them" (Ps. 103:17ff)?

"To those who keep his covenant. . . ." This is why Timothy heard the Scriptures, and saw them illustrated in his home, even from his infancy. Keeping the covenant means that "you shall love the Lord your God with all your heart and with all your soul and with all your strength. And these words which I am commanding you today, shall be on your heart, and you shall teach them diligently to your sons and shall talk of them when you sit in your house and when you walk by the way and when you lie down and when you rise up" (Deut. 6:5ff.).

No wonder Timothy believed that Jesus was the Messiah. He had been reared in an atmosphere of faith in the Scriptures, and the Scriptures led Timothy to Jesus. "To children's children"—from Lois, to Eunice, to Timothy. "I have been reminded of your sincere faith, which first lived in your grandmother Lois and in your mother Eunice, and I am persuaded, now lives in you also" (II Tim. 1:5).

Faith begets faith, on the human level. This is the promise of God who kept the covenant and Timothy became a believer. Likewise, if we enthusiastically serve the Lord in faith, our children and pupils will have the opportunity to catch this enthusiasm.

But there were others who also taught the Scriptures. Their teaching brought their disciples into bondage! They took away "the key to knowledge" (Luke 11:52). We call them lawyers, scribes, rulers of the people. They too had enthusiasm but it was misdirected; it was not born of faith. The wonderful law of God, revealed through Moses and the prophets, had become for them not a message of God's deliverance but a means of self-deliverance.

There are products of Christian schools today who hate their schools, and hate the Lord of those schools. To hear them tell it, Christian education was a method to stifle, repress, and deaden; Christian teachers were at best, unfulfilled legalists working out their salvation with arrogance and cruelty; at worst, they were neurotics creating a world which did not exist and certainly was not the world described in the Scriptures.

We must not forget what the Scriptures are. They are not at the heart a list of do's and don'ts; they are a divinely-given means of grace. Even the negatives have their gracious side: "Twas grace that taught my heart to fear, and grace that fear relieved." Hence no commandment should be separated from God's gracious purpose to bring us to Christ and to cause us to share in his glory. This means that a Christian school must not become a "reform school," or an institution where civic virtues are taught. It must always be an extenstion of a Christian home, a place where keeping the covenant is the dominant mood or atmosphere, where righteousness and holiness are essentials of the curriculum, and the power of God is counted on as the only dynamic for Christian living.

We should note that the things Paul cherished in Timothy were not externals, but were matters of the heart. Enthusiasm in the service of the Lord was not generated by mere conformity to external norms. Similarly, Christian schools should aim to cultivate, not so much outward conformity to the mores of society, but the inner disposition of holiness and integrity. Of course, conformity in a Christian is important, but so is non-conformity! Any outward conformity has its dangers in hypocrisy and superficiality.

Many Christian parents see their children as extensions of their own personalities, and whatever else happens they hope that their children will not disgrace them with their neighbors. Hence, the great stress on outward conformity. One wonders, however, about the parents of John the Baptist. One can imagine the conversations which took place in their village as the children were growing up: one might have boasted that his son was making it in the fish business; another might have boasted that his son was excelling in the study of law in Jerusalem. But ask Elizabeth and Zacharias how John was doing, and their response had to be, "O, he's out in the desert eating locusts and wild honey!" Yet John was where God wanted him, and his parents would have had every reason to be proud of him.

Outward conformity leads to hypocrisy, and that sin is high on God's list of things he hates. A remarkable verse is found in Jeremiah 3: "Faithless Israel has proved herself

23

more righteous than treacherous Judah" (v. 11). One need only recall Old Testament history to see what an amazing judgment God was making. Israel was really faithless; she worshipped the wrong god at the wrong place with the help of the wrong priests. She had fallen to unbelief quickly under Jeroboam and that apostasy continued for centuries despite the ministries of such prophets as Elijah and Elisha.

Judah, by contrast, was a good nation; she worshipped at the appointed place with the help of legitimate priests, and experienced several revivals under the leadership of good kings and faithful prophets. Surely if we had to make a choice we would have chosen Judah despite all her faults. But God didn't! "Faithless Israel has proved herself more righteous than treacherous Judah." Judah's treachery is spelled out in the verse which precedes: "And yet in spite of all this her treacherous sister Judah did not return to me with all her heart, but rather in deception." God hates hypocrisy even more than unbelief, especially when it is the people of God who are the hypocrites.

When Christian parents and Christian schools overstress conformity to cultural norms they may be inducing the sin of treachery in their young people, and those same young people may have to unlearn the principles of conformity if they are to obey God's command, "Be not conformed to this world, but be transformed." Oh, that today's generation might present their minds and bodies wholeheartedly as living sacrifices in the spiritual service of worship to Christ!

4. Timothy, the Pupil Trained to Expose Falsehood and Teach Truth.

But there was another lesson in Timothy's life which has a bearing on the purpose and program of Christian education. Timothy was trained to *expose falsehood and teach the truth.* During his early years he was subject to the discipline of his mother and grandmother, and later was an apprentice missionary and evangelist with the Apostle Paul. Soon, however, the time was to come that he would be "on his

24

own," pastoring several congregations in Asia, giving leadership to the churches while Paul himself was in prison or engaged in evangelism elsewhere.

To complete his education, Paul wrote Timothy two letters of counsel and admonition. Although Timothy was well versed in the gospel, he also needed to know about false teachers, and false teachings (cf. I Tim. 1:3-7, 18-20; 4:1-6; 6:3-5; II Tim. 2:17-21; 3:1-9; 4:3-5). Just as a bank teller must be skilled in detecting counterfeit currency, so Timothy had to be aware of the kinds of false doctrines which were in the world in his day. He had to be aware of them for his own sake, but also as a faithful pastor he also had to protect the flock from the false shepherds (I Tim. 4:6, 16). Moreover, he needed to preach and teach so that the false teachers themselves might be persuaded of the truth (II Tim. 2:24-26).

There is a sense in which Timothy had an easier time of it than the child of God today. Not only have the false doctrines multiplied since the days of the apostles, but the means of dissemination are much more numerous and more readily available. All the more reason then that Christian homes and schools must prepare young people for an intelligent defense of the gospel, an awareness of the forms which unbelief is taking these days, and a compassion for false teachers "that they may come to their senses and escape from the trap of the devil, who has taken them captive to do his will (II Tim. 2:26).

Just as Paul instructed Timothy regarding the enemies of the cross both within the church and outside of it, so a pupil in a Christian school today must be aware of the errors of our day. Of course, the teaching must be adapted to the level of maturity of the student, but in his formative years he must be made aware that there is an enemy, and that the Christian is called to warfare.

The men of Issachar ought to be the example for modern Christians. The chronicler wrote that they were "men who understood the times, with knowledge of what Israel should do" (I Chron. 12:32). Now an understanding of the times certainly includes, first of all, a knowledge of Scripture and of Scripture's prophecies. Only when we view the world from the vantage point of the Bible can we assume to know what is happening in our day.

But in God's providence our world is being shaped by the ideas and desires of wicked men and we cannot understand our times without some understanding of what these men said and wrote. Just to name a few—our thinking today is permeated by the ideas of Hume, Freud, Darwin, Marx, Dewey, and Kant. The Christian student today, even on the elementary level, should begin to understand where these men went astray and why, and he should see how subtly their views have crept into the thinking of all of us when we watch TV, read a news magazine, or have a friendly chat with our neighbor.

In this connection, I should point out that a study of false views infecting our society today, conducted under the leadership of a sensitive teacher, can be quite therapeutic. Indeed, wrong ideas continue to permeate the thinking of those Christians for whom our culture, or way of life, means more to them than the commandments of Scripture. This is not only a problem of our day; it has always been a problem for the people of God and was even one of the burdens of the prophets of Israel.

Some Christians are alive to this issue, but there are also some who have surrendered to our culture without a fight. A young lady came into my office some years ago to say that the contents of a particular course were above her. I pointed out that they were supposed to be—the course was a "mind-stretcher" to make a freshman aware of the problems and opportunities of our day—and then asked her whether such things as current events were topics of discussion at home. She sighed and said that her parents never discussed things like that, let alone tried to view them from a biblical perspective. "What do they talk about?," I made the mistake of asking. However, her reply was informative, "Other people."

We become Christians, Paul wrote, by "the renewing of

26

our minds," and the contemporary Christian student may well receive this renewal in class, in chapel, and by homework assignments, but perhaps we need a revival of "tabletalk" in which parents deliberately discuss such things about the evening table. Perhaps then we will have a modern example of Moses' word to parents that they should teach their sons God's commandments "when you sit in your house, and when you walk by the way."

But Paul also wanted Timothy prepared for life within the Christian community. The first epistle especially was written with this in mind (3:15). For all its weaknesses and errors, it is the Christian community which is responsible to witness for Christ within the world today. Someone has remarked jokingly but with a ring of truth to it, that the church has to be supernatural, otherwise with all its failings it would have disappeared from the face of the earth long ago.

But the weaknesses of the church must be corrected and they must be corrected by people. They can be corrected by people only as young people are made aware of God's plan and purpose for the church in particular and for the Christian community in general.

The Christian community must regain its place of centrality in the minds and hearts of Christian people today. In a sense it is too bad that the "neighborhood church" is no longer a reality. Often members of a church live many miles from each other and from the place of worship, with their fellowship limited to a very few hours each week. Far different the life of the early church who broke bread from house to house and from day to day! It is difficult to bear another's burdens when you see the other so infrequently and so briefly, and when friendships are more permanent in non-Christian contexts.

Hence we Christians today need to hear God's Word regarding the whole of our lives so that a sense of community can be recovered. In Timothy's day, the believers were instructed about marriage (I Tim. 4:3), diet (4:3, 4), interpersonal relations (5:1-16), management and labor relations (6:1-2), and the use of money (6:6-10, 17-19). Because God was the Lord over all, and his Word was the rule of both faith and life the Christians were drawn together, and in the multiplicity made their impact on the world outside.

Like Timothy, prepared by Paul to serve Christ in the church and in the outside world, young people today must see the breadth and depth of the claims which the sovereign God rightly has over their lives. All of this cannot be done within the context of the Christian school. In fact, it will be the greater responsibility of the home and the church to implement this preparation; yet the school, if it is to produce present day Timothys, must take the whole counsel of God into account.

Here then is an ideal towards which every Christian home and every Christian school must strive—to train Timothys for the task of working in the church and in the world. Unless our young people have a genuine concern for others, are Christ-centered in their whole approach to living and thinking, and show an enthusiasm for the work of God's kingdom, and are trained to expose falsehood and teach the truth, we shall fail in our witness to this generation.

The Instruction of the Bible

1. The Necessity of a Biblical Education/Curriculum

It is at this point that we leave Timothy as our example, and move towards a consideration of what the Bible says about Christian education in general and about a school's curriculum in particular. Prior to this, however, we must look at a common objection to Christian schools as the God-appointed vehicle for Christian education. Timothy himself did not receive a Christian school education. Commentators are careful to point out that there was probably no synagogue in Lystra and therefore no synagogue school. Whatever formal education he may have received must have been pagan. Likewise, the two greatest leaders in the Bible were educated in unbelieving surroundings—"Moses was educated in all the wisdom of the Egyptians and was powerful in speech and action" (Acts 7:22); Paul was educated at the feet of Gamaliel, ". . . in regard to the law, a Pharisee, as for zeal, persecuting the church; as for legal righteousness, faultless" (Phil. 3:5, 6).

These examples do make a point, that all is not lost if a Christian school is not at hand. Perhaps they also point out that Christian schools are not for every child and in all circumstances. But they can be made to prove too much, and they do overlook some important truths about the lives of Moses and Paul. To Moses God was most emphatic: "You shall not do what is done in the land of Egypt where you lived, nor are you to do what is done in the land of Canaan where I am bringing you; you shall not walk in their statutes" (Deut. 18:3). Whatever Moses had learned in the court of Pharaoh, he was to unlearn in the wilderness![1] Similarly, Paul came to the place where he considered all his former training as "loss for the sake of Christ" (Phil. 3:7). Whatever Paul learned in Tarsus and at the feet of Gamaliel, he had to unlearn in the school of Christ!

This too applies to Christian schools. They must not just take any secular curriculum and sanctify it by a chapel program, a course in Bible, and a prayer before each class. Moses had to learn "My statutes"; Paul had to "consider everything as loss compared to the surpassing greatness of knowing Christ Jesus my Lord" (Phil. 3:8).

There is an old saying that a preacher needs two books: the Bible and the roll book of the congregation he serves. The point is that he serves best who knows not only the Bible but also the needs of his people to whom he must apply the Bible's teachings. Similarly, a Christian school curriculum must grow out of an understanding of God's world as that understanding is molded by the Scriptures, and out of an understanding of the teachers and pupils and what the Bible

---

1. Geerhardus Vos, in his excellent study, *Biblical Theology*, makes this point on pp. 115 ff.

says to them.[2] There are Christian schools which give lip service to Christian education, but Skinner, Dewey, and Marx have crept in unawares and the Bible is taught in a context in which both student and teacher have no concern for what the Bible says to them as pupil and educator.

For example, many schools today view the educative process as the transmission of the teacher's knowledge to the eager students. The teacher is the authority not only for conduct but also for knowledge. How differently did God view that same process in Deuteronomy 6. The Word of God was taught in the crucible of human experience. The child learned the Scriptures as his parents worked in the house, and walked in the way. The child saw his parents struggle with problems.

When I was a youngster my father gave me some tools: plane, vise, saw, and the like. I turned out some pretty miserable pieces of woodwork. A neighbor once discussed this with my father in my presence. He said, "Billy [his son] watches me saw and he saws." My father who was a physician had no interest in carpentry, and I had no example to follow.

Later on, when I was en route to college, we had an auto accident. No one was hurt but we were all shaken up. The father of one of my friends calmly reached for his Bible, read Psalm 23, and then prayed for us. I had known that was the thing to do, but it wasn't real until that accident. I watched him read and pray, and so I learned to read and pray.

When present day students see some of that struggle in their parents and teachers, they will learn more about God and the world from watching the struggle than from just carefully putting lecture thoughts into their notebooks, to be reproduced (and forgotten!) on a quiz later on in the term.

This point is important because of the nature of Christian education. Its goal is the glory of God; specifically, to help a child develop his God-given talents to the full and to use

2. Christian school board members, teachers, and parents will benefit from a study, *To Those Who Teach* by a former colleague, Geraldine Steensma.

these talents to glorify God. The key words are "develop" and "use." Most curricula have little outlet for development and use. These are confined to extra-curricular activities such as soccer, band, and the annual play. *These* talents are developed and used, but they are *extra*-curricular, while the curriculum goes its merry way with the child passively absorbing what the teacher, or the textbook, says with little opportunity for development and use.

But even before talents are developed and used, they must be identified. Many Christian schools, doubtless because of the ever present economic factors, are geared to the student whose talents are of a highly intellectual nature, and have no place for identifying (to say nothing of developing and using) talents such as carpentry, typing, and data processing. Yet God is the giver of all talents, and none is to be despised. Yet by example, we seem to be teaching that God is more interested in history and mathematics than he is in "manual training."

The point of all these remarks is that boards, faculties, and parents must study the curriculum with their Bibles in their hands, putting to good use the insights which God gave to the world centuries ago but which have fallen into discard as people began to go their own humanistic way.

Now some of these insights may be superficially like certain false teachings. For example, the "development" and "use" mentioned above may be interpreted by some to be Dewey's "learning by doing" under another name. Of course, a Christian school will reject the humanistic assumptions of Dewey's pragmatism. However, this is not to say that all "learning by doing" is humanistic. In fact, when we survey the history of God's people in the Old Testament, we see that God frequently taught his people by giving them things to do. The substitutionary atonement is most clearly taught not in the propositions of the New Testament but in the sacrifices of the Old. And Paul says that the command to pay your preacher is imbedded in the command not to muzzle the ox when he is treading out the corn (cf. I Cor. 9:8-10).

There are humanists who oppose Dewey's "learning by doing." They are no closer to the Scriptures than Dewey himself. Christians must therefore not make choices among various educators today, seeking to choose from the teaching a little here, a little there. Rather, we must search the Scriptures and learn from God not only what to teach but also how to teach it.

Until the American Christian community produces textbooks for its Christian schools, we may have to rely on some of the productions of humanist publishing houses. But we must be sensitive to the philosophies which underlie even the simplest of reading books.

A good many years ago I was asked to teach a course in "Christian education" to a number of women who had enrolled in a theological seminary. Several of these young women were themselves graduates of teachers' colleges, and I certainly did not want to compete with them in the subject matter of the course! So we studied the Scriptures to find not only the assumptions of pedagogy, but also the methods. At the end of the course, one of the young women came to say that I had forced her to rethink *everything* she had learned in teacher's college, things which she had unwittingly assumed were sound principles because they had seemed "all right" to her.

2. The Impossibility of a Biblical Curriculum

When I was dean of the faculty of Covenant College,[3] I used to tell our faculty that their task was more difficult than that of teachers in colleges where no Christian commitment was expected. We would have to go further and place all facts in Christian context.

---

3. A Christian college affiliated with the Reformed Presbyterian Church Evangelical Synod, and the Presbyterian Church in America, located in Lookout Mountain, Tennessee.

This same thought now emerges from what I have written above. To be a Christian school teacher or a Christian school board member is a difficult task indeed and requires many more hours than might be expected of others in similar positions. Perhaps I can best state what I am trying to say by putting it this way: we cannot really have a Christian school until first of all we realize that humanly speaking it is impossible. In writing this I am not trying to be overly dramatic. I am seeking once again to be guided by the Scriptures.

When Joshua was giving his farewell address to Israel, he wanted to stress the importance of their keeping the covenant. He certainly did it in a very strange way. He said, "You will not be able to serve the Lord, for He is a Holy God" (Josh. 24:19). Joshua understood that the secret to true obedience, in contrast to superficial and outward obedience, lies in knowing that it is impossible apart from the grace of God.

The Provision of God

1. The Provision of Godly Wisdom

This brings us then to the provision God has made for teaching his Word. The Jewish scribes had a saying that God spent one quarter of each day in the synagogue teaching the children. They put it this way in order to show how important the training of children was. As a statement of fact, it is probably not far from the truth.

There are a number of Old Testament words which describe God's provision for an education which is biblical: *wisdom, discretion,* and *discipline* are a few of them. They are the key words of the Book of Proverbs and there is no real understanding of that book apart from a grasp of these words. Boards and faculties would do well to study Proverbs in their meetings, because the "wisdom" of the Bible is quite different from the wisdom of Athens and other cultural centers.

33

Wisdom is from above; it is not essentially an earthly subject. In fact, it begins with the fear of the Lord (read Job 28), and it is nurtured in the atmosphere of the fear of the Lord. This is the key to knowledge: knowledge is not the accumulation of facts (although a considerable part of it is just that) but knowledge begins in an attitude with which no human being is born; every human being who gets it must get it from God by a supernatural work. Christian education cannot thrive except in an atmosphere which understands human limitations and looks to God for wisdom, for the fear which is the beginning of wisdom, and for the continuing state of mind which Paul describes in II Corinthians 10:5: "We are destroying speculations and every lofty thing raised up against the knowledge of God, and we are taking every thought captive to the obedience of Christ."

2. The Provision of a Godly Atmosphere

These thoughts should indicate that Christian education is not a part time task. The pupil cannot come to school, adopt a "fear of the Lord" attitude as he walks through the door, and leave it at the door when he goes home. There can be no education apart from sanctification for everyone (from janitor to school board president) who contributes to this atmosphere.

It is at this point that a vexing question raises its head. Should Christian schools admit as pupils the children of non-Christian homes? A corollary is, what place does evangelism have in a Christian school? A certain amount of realism is needed to face these questions. First, children from Christian homes are not "angels." While in many of them the grace of God has already worked to give them new life, there are others who are still strangers to that grace.[4] Hence, evangelism must go on within the walls of a Christian school. But,

---

4. The holiness of I Corinthians 7:14 and the promises of Acts 2:39 are not guarantees of personal sanctification.

second, it is a mistake to separate education and evangelism as though they were two distinct things. When the Bible is properly taught, Jesus Christ is the theme of each chapter and each verse. He brought this truth home to his disciples in Luke 24: "And beginning with Moses and all the Prophets, he explained to them what was said in all the Scriptures concerning himself" (v. 27).

But the question about the admission of believers must be answered in the context of "atmosphere." Students make the atmosphere of a school; in far more ways than we realize, they teach each other, and what they teach may be quite opposite to the position of the school. And as noted above, while non-believers and especially ones from non-believing homes may indeed infect the atmosphere with humanism, believing children who are not yet fully sanctified may do the same.

Christian schools are frequently blamed when some of their students reject the faith. Yet sometimes the reason is beyond the control of the school. I know of a young man who became a skeptic during his college days, not because of any error taught in his courses, but because of racist attitudes of churches in the community.

In a more positive vein—some of us in our college dorm came to grasp certain biblical truths, not because of any specific teaching in classes but because of what was talked about in the "rap sessions" held in the dormitory. The men with whom I discussed things provided the Christian atmosphere I learned in.

Atmosphere is not something which can be settled by an admissions policy, or even by careful screening by an admissions committee; it is a prevailing problem which must be faced each day the school is open. Hence, frequent personal contacts must be made by board members and teachers with students, and of course this will be one of the highest of prayer priorities for all the Christian community.

Atmosphere too has its extremes. In searching for it, a Christian school may find itself tending in the direction of

35

extreme isolation and monasticism. It must always be kept in mind that the pupil is being prepared for life in the world, and in that world he cannot depend on continual support from a Christian community. He must learn, and must be taught, to face unbelief and unbelievers in the marketplace as a responsible Christian. That marketplace must not be caricatured or misrepresented. Many a graduate of a Christian school has come to the opinion that he has been misled by his Christian teachers—either the world was worse than he had been led to believe, or much better. In either case, there is disillusionment and perhaps defection from the faith.

Christian schools must not be discouraged by failure, either. There have been some notable instances where Christian schools have not only failed in their objective, they have in fact achieved the very opposite. Moreover, every Christian school will have its minor failures and defeats along the way. The real issue is not that there has been failure, but rather whether and how the school has reacted to that failure so that the whole community benefits from it. It should also be borne in mind that failures make news; successes, especially in education, don't. Many pupils have graduated every year to serve God in this world, but we hear little of them when Christian education is discussed.

The Encouragement to Persevere

One final word of commandment and encouragement. Christian schools frequently choose Proverbs 22:6 as their motto. It is an apt one, especially when it is properly understood. One commentator, Franz Delitzsch, translates it, and then makes the comment: "Give to the child instruction conformable to his way? So he will not when he becomes old, depart from it. . . ." The education of youth ought to be conformed to the nature of youth; the matter of instruction, the manner of instruction, ought to regulate itself according to the stage of life, and its peculiarities; the method ought to be arranged according to the degree of

36

development which the mental and bodily life of the youth has arrived at."[5]

The proverb calls to our attention that young people are growing and their education should be adapted to their degree of maturity. This means, among other things, that adult reactions and conduct should not be expected and required of young people. They should not be treated as adults until they are. A mother once approached me about her "backslidden" son and she wanted me to speak with him about this. He was in an elementary school and gave every evidence of growing up to be a fine Christian. Yet in his mother's eyes he was "backslidden." He had made a decision to become a foreign missionary in a meeting held in his church. This was a number of months ago. Yet, when there had been a fire in a house down the street the week preceding, he had rushed home with the word that he wanted to be a fireman! This was his backsliding.

Faithfulness and perseverance in our promises is certainly a Christian characteristic, and in adults it is something which has moral overtones. But a lad of ten or less can certainly be granted a passing whim, especially when fire engines are down the street!

The same commentator continues that the training of youth in conformity with his nature which is imprinted and inbred and to which he becomes accustomed is that training from which he will not depart.

This is not a promise based on statistics or the law of averages; it is the promise of a sovereign God and "a suitable motto for the lesson books of pedagogues and catechists."

---

5. Dr. Jay Adams, in *Competent to Counsel* (page 158) offers an alternative to this quote from Delitzsch, maintaining that to bring up a child "in the way he should go" is to let the child go his own way rather than God's way.—Editor.

Chapter 3
TEACHER

The Purpose of a Christian School Is . . .

That the Teacher Relate the Bible to
What Is Taught in the Classroom

NOEL K. WEEKS*

It Is Possible!

Does the Bible relate to what is taught in the classroom?
Many would say it has no relation to modern education,
although the reasons for saying that vary. Often the reasons
given for denying the relevance of the Bible are themselves
very good proof of its relevance. Let us look at some of these
arguments.

1. The Argument that the Bible Is Obsolete

The argument stated: The Bible was written during various
times in the past. The Bible was written in terms of the
beliefs and customs of its day. Those beliefs and customs are
obviously different from the ones we now follow. Hence the
Bible has nothing to say to our day.

*Dr. Noel K. Weeks is presently a lecturer in history at the University of Sydney, Australia. He has provided leadership as secretary of a newly founded Christian school in the Sydney area. His broad background includes a University B.S. degree, B.D. and Th.M. degrees from Westminster Seminary, and M.A. and Ph.D. degrees (Mediterranean Studies) from Brandeis University. His publications include *Early River Civilizations*, a student textbook written for Pergamon Press.

Response: This is not an argument against the relevance of the Bible to the classroom. It is an argument against the whole Christian faith. The argument claims that what is "true" in one period of history is not necessarily "true" in any other period. That position is known as historical relativism. The person who holds to this belief will reject anything from the past. However, God's Word is and remains true. The assurance that Jesus gives to us is that his words will not pass away (Matt. 24:35).

Our rejection of historical relativism will affect our teaching. It will affect, for example, the way we teach history. History is not just a chaos of changing opinions and customs with no standard by which we may judge whether change is good or bad. Thus this objection is really proof that the Bible is relevant because even in rejecting the Bible the argument borrows from *a Christian view of history.*

The argument restated: Only certain things in the Bible were written in terms of the beliefs and customs of the time. When the Bible talks about Christ and our salvation then what it says is true for all time. But when it talks about the natural world, history, etc., it is using the ideas of the time and is not an authority for us who have different ideas. Thus where the Bible touches on school subjects it is not an authority for us.

Response: This is an argument for dualism. It says that the Bible is our source for "religious" truth but we have to go elsewhere for "secular" truth. We are thus left with a double, or dual standard with which to judge supposedly different types of truth. Dualism makes a distinction between our knowledge of God's salvation and our knowledge of God's creation and providence. Colossians rejects that dualism. It rejects it because Christ is the head of creation, providence *and* redemption. In Colossians 1:15-20 Paul points out that Christ is Lord and creator of the old and new creation. He upholds his old creation and his newly created church. In 1:9 and 2:3 he points out that Christ is the source of all wisdom. Then in 2:8ff. he makes use of what he has already taught to refute the view that there is another source of authority in human tradition or philosophy. If Christ is the Lord of all then there is nothing in *all* creation that may stand alongside of him as a source of wisdom. If Christ as Lord of creation and providence has all wisdom, how can we say that we cannot learn about the creation from his Word?

Another version of the argument: The Bible was written in terms of a particular set of beliefs and customs. God controls the development of human culture. We have different beliefs and customs because God has so ordained it. We should not be surprised that the Bible no longer applies today. We do not keep many of the laws that Moses gave to Israel. These laws are now obsolete. So, while some very general principles may remain, changes in culture have made many specific biblical teachings and commandments obsolete.

Response: The first part of the argument is that God controls whatever comes to pass. The conclusion is then made that the culture of the modern world must be good because God so ordained it. The argument ignores the force of Romans 1. God does govern but he governs in wrath as well as mercy. When men refuse the truth, God delivers them to greater and greater sinfulness. If we simply take over and adopt the culture of our times, we may be adopting the products of men hardened in their sin.

God's law in the Bible is not changed just to accomodate for a change in beliefs or customs. God's law does not bow to human custom. It demands that man bow to it. There is a change in law only when God, by an act of redemption, brings his people into a new situation for which a new law is appropriate. A good example is provided by comparing Leviticus 17:3-6 and Deuteronomy 12. The first passage states that while in the wilderness Israel had to slaughter their cattle *at the doorway of the tabernacle.* In Deuteronomy 12, however, Israel looks foward to the day when they will enter the land of the promise. When God extends their borders as he has promised them (v. 20), then there will be a new situation. In that new situation a new rule will apply and those living far from the central place of worship will be able to butcher their cattle at the home where they live.

The same applies to the changes in certain regulations that come with Christ. When God, by his salvation, creates a new situation for his people, he gives them new and appropriate regulations. In many ways the situation will not change. Thus, while the new situation brought by Christ does *not* make murder, adultery, etc., right, it *does* mean that we no longer gather at a place of worship in earthly Jerusalem.

The next act of redemption that is promised is the return of Christ. We therefore should not expect to see any change in the commands we obey until our Lord comes again. (See appendix I for the discussion of some further problems.)

This point has implications for our school teaching. What happens when the Bible makes a statement in the area of science or social order? Is its relevance dismissed because the Bible was speaking to a former age that was prescientific and not socially differentiated? If it is, then the division of history on social or technological grounds is being taken as more important than the division based upon God's redemption.[1]

We do not deny that other changes are going on in history beside the changes brought about by God's acts of redemption. There are social, technological and ideological changes. However, if the Bible is still our authority we may assess, and if necessary, reject these changes in the light of God's Word. As soon as we give up the authority of the Bible in our day

1. To understand history we need some way of distinguishing the major eras. The tendency today is to teach history as primarily the history of human progress. If the emphasis is on scientific accomplishments then the major "eras" of history will be divided by new discoveries or techniques. So we will see the major division as being between our "scientific/technological" age and the former "prescientific" age. Indeed people are thinking this way when they believe that a Bible written in a "prescientific" age cannot be an authority today.

41

we make ourselves prisoners in this present age, conformed to the pattern of this world.

2. The Textbook Argument

The argument: The Bible is not a "textbook." It does not give us all the principles and information we need for teaching all the subjects.

Response: The same charge that the Bible is incomplete might be raised in any other area. Basically, the argument is this: to say anything the Bible must say everything.

The argument restated: More pointedly stated the Bible does not have the form of a textbook. If God wanted us to use the Bible in our subjects, he would have written it in the form of a textbook.

Response: This is a form of the argument that the "Bible is obsolete" which we treated above. It requires that the Bible conform to the pattern of a modern textbook if it is to say anything in the academic disciplines.

The premise behind the argument is that truth must come with a certain sort of wrapping. Scientific truth, for example, must be presented in a certain form. The reason for this expectation will be considered later. Yet the observation should be made that we have become accustomed to truth being presented in one form and one form only. If the Bible does not wear the external appearance of a textbook of science or history, then it is regarded as without relevance in these areas. Yet, because Christ, as Lord of science and history, has all wisdom, we can say that we will learn about the creation from his Word.

Use the Scriptures!

The issues raised in the preceding section require more extensive discussion. In theory we may hold that the Bible should be our authority in all areas of life, but we find difficulty in putting that into practice. Let us examine how

42

we should proceed to use the Scriptures in Christian education.

1. The Words of Scripture

We have all seen examples of a few words of Scripture plucked from context to defend error and stupidity. In reaction to this there is a tendency to direct our appeal to the general principles of Scripture rather than specific passages. The danger that lies in appeal to principles is that sometimes the principles because so vague as to be meaningless. Indeed, at times we will find "biblical principles" advocated which are at variance with specific statements of Scripture. We should not set "words" and "principles" at variance with each other. If we study the words and phrases of Scripture, we find new and fresh truths. When Christ was confronted by the Sadducean argument against the resurrection (Matt. 22:23-33) he did not appeal to a "textbook" treatment of the resurrection. He appealed to a passage which was primarily concerned with another issue, quoting: "I am the God of Abraham, the God of Isaac, and the God of Jacob." Nevertheless, in this terminology of Scripture to be "the God of" is a phrase which indicates that a covenant exists between God and that person. But God cannot be in covenant with the nonexistent dead (Luke 20:38). Hence the patriarchs Abraham, Isaac, and Jacob must live forever. Although the resurrection may not have been the central point of the passage in Exodus 3:15, which Christ quoted, God could not have used this rich covenant term in identifying himself to Moses at the burning bush if the human parties in the covenant had ceased to exist. It is a just and necessary inference from this that the dead live and shall continue to live on.

The point of the illustration is that Jesus did not need a textbook passage on the resurrection to prove his point. Jesus speaks out of deep sensitivity to the biblical use of words. If we are condemned because, in our search for principles and instructions in our teaching, we appeal to passages not primarily or originally directed to Christian school teachers, then Jesus is also condemned.

Does this open the door for the worst sort of "proof-texting"? Not at all, because the meaning of the phrase "I am the God of . . ." comes from the recurrent biblical use of that and similar phrases. Our context is all of Scripture.

Similarly Paul appeals in Colossians to the cosmic significance of Christ, as the Lord and head of creation, in order to ban any turning to angels or human traditions as an alternative source of wisdom apart from the apostolic revelation. Surely it is a legitimate inference that there is no other alternative source in the creation from which we are to obtain the fulness of wisdom and knowledge.

2. Testing the Results

Jesus rejects the Pharisaic system of tradition because it leads to results contrary to Scripture (Matt. 15:1-9). The great legalistic system created by the Pharisees is tested by Scripture and found wanting. Paul refutes the rejection of the resurrection because of the ethical consequences of denial (I Cor. 15:30-33). Systems and beliefs should be tested by their fruits.

Can this principle be abused? The test must be Scripture and not some assumed logical absurdity. As we have just seen in our discussion of Matthew 22:23-33, the Sadducees were in one sense testing the belief in resurrection. However, the touchstone was not Scripture; it was human logic. And thus it assumed that the present situation with its marrying and giving in marriage would determine the future age rather than the power of God.

When human systems are submitted to the test of Scripture, there is resistance. Men are very proud of their great systems. Should such a magnificent intellectual achievement be rejected just because the results are at variance with Scripture? Often the defense is not put in this form. It will be argued or implied that we cannot reject this system until we have something at least as comprehensive to take its place. Thus the test of truth is no longer Scripture. Instead, apparent intellectual complexity, completeness and sophistication become the text. (See appendix IV.)

Of course Jesus and Paul, in the examples given above, do set forth the true position after having rejected the false. They do not defend their positions as being more extensive, sophisticated and comprehensive. They defend them as the truth of God.

3. Know and Do

It is the consistent testimony of Scripture that there cannot be true knowledge and right conduct without inner righteousness (Prov. 1:7; 4:23-27; John 8:31-59). We must reject any system which claims to lay bare the secrets of the universe to believer and unbeliever equally and alike. Truth is not known apart from a right relationship of the heart to God. The truth of Scripture cannot be known and embraced apart from the work of God's Spirit in the heart. This means that in making the Scripture our standard we are not presenting a set of pat formulas. We will have to struggle to understand and apply the teaching of Scripture because of the effects of sin on us.

One of the faults of non-Christian systems is that they claim to be able to reveal the truth to men regardless of the state of their hearts. Unfortunately, Christians taking a dualistic approach often adopt these non-Christian systems. For instance, it will be argued by some that the scientist is concerned merely with the creation and not with God. But, according to Scripture that very separation between concern with God and concern with the creation comes from the rejection of the truth. Romans 1 teaches that man should recognize from the creation the power and deity of the God who made it. His failure to do so is due to a refusal to have God in his knowledge (Rom. 1:21). We are so conditioned by our own sinfulness, and by a Christian community that has accepted dualism, that we too often view creation without acknowledging a Creator.

To return to a right understanding we must obey the Word of God. There is no great theoretical system that will be revealed to us whether or not we are willing to put the Word of God into practice. It is a matter of obedience to what we now know and the deeper understanding that comes as we struggle to do the truth (John 8:31, 32).

The Bible is not written in the form of a "textbook," but that does not mean it says nothing to the academic disciplines, because a mere collection of facts and truths is very inadequate for all of life. We require also the exhortation and the incentive to *live* by truth.

4. Rejection of Allegory

As far back as Philo in the first century A.D. there have been attempts to accommodate the Scriptures to pagan philosophies. Generally it is argued that the Bible was written to the nonphilosophical and the nonintellectual. Such readers grasp only the surface meaning of the Bible while the philosophically intelligent person finds hints that there is another level of meaning. The wise and philosophical can read these hints as pointing to their treasured intellectual system.

This is really another form of dualism. Although they claim to have discovered another level of meaning, the philosophical system is not really taught by the Bible. It is read into the Bible by artibrarily assigning meanings to biblical words. The meanings and concepts assigned are derived from pagan systems of thought. Since the Bible is not philosophical, it is denied the right to judge the philosophical system. The system may be imposed on Scripture but Scripture is denied the right to pass judgement upon it.

In our day there is a common variation of this dualistic method. The evolutionary approach to human culture is combined with an allegorical use of the biblical text. It is claimed that Scripture, written in an earlier state of human development, cannot be expected to teach the philosophical or scientific system involved. It contains, of course, anticipations and hints which the man who has embraced the true system will know how to read. But Scripture may not judge the system.

Here a false view of the history of revelation is combined with a dualism. Once Scripture is given the right to pass judgment on the human system, the deviations of human thought can be detected and the system challenged. As long as Scripture is denied that right, there is no way to prevent autonomous human thought from dominating the whole system. Certainly every system will put forward tests of truth and claim that it passes its own test. But our tests should be God's and not our own.

Can we avoid imposing our own concepts of Scripture? Only the painstaking method of comparing Scripture with Scripture will detect such impositions. This is not a mere intellectual exercise, but a spiritual struggle, for our own pride and the influence of the spirit of this world make us want to suppress the Biblical data which does not fit into our system.

The problem is not basically the psychological problem that we find what we expect to find. If it were merely that, then we would have the excuse that the structure of our minds makes it difficult or impossible for us to receive new truth. We could excuse our conformity to the world. The problem is that of the proud and sinful human mind. Therefore we are responsible to use the God-given means to bring all our thoughts and ideas into subjection to God's Word. There is no instantaneous intellectual sanctification. There are moments when new truths become clear and cause us to reshape our ideas but even these new ideas must be subjected to the refinement of Scripture.

5. The Scripture Is Sufficient for the Classroom

Is the Bible comprehensive enough to be our standard in all of life? We have already seen the tendency to make "completeness" the measure of truth. There is a reluctance to

47

reject an elaborate system simply because it contradicts Scripture. When this same mentality looks at the Scripture, it immediately judges the Scripture as being insufficiently detailed. Hence the Scripture is rejected because it is incomplete.

We must realize that this "incompleteness" is not restricted to what the Bible says about science or history. Even in theology or ethics it does not say everything. God has not revealed everything to man (Deut. 29:29). Man is not God and his knowledge is not the same as God's knowledge (Ps. 139:6). The systems of unbelieving men attempt to put man in the place of God. Hence they take as their ideal the comprehensive and total knowledge that is God's alone. When the Bible does not come up to their "divine" standard, it is rejected, or has to be supplemented by human philosophy or tradition.

Yet the problem remains as to how the Bible is to be our authority in all the many varied situations of life. As mentioned above, this is just as much a problem in ethics as in science. The Bible is a sufficient rule for godly conduct (Deut. 30:8-20; II Tim. 3:14-17) and yet it does not give a detailed rule for every conceivable circumstance. It is instructive to study the structure of biblical law. We find both general principles and specific legislation. For example we find a law concerning stealing (Exod. 20:15). And we find more detailed outworkings of this law (Exod. 22). We find that failure to take adequate precautions to safeguard another's property is a form of stealing (22:5, 6).

This rule raises the question of what are to be considered adequate provisions to safeguard the property of another, especially in the case where property has been entrusted to someone for safekeeping (22:7-13). The rules with regard to safekeeping have to be distinguished from those in the case of borrowing. Borrowing, in general, implies the obligation to return what was borrowed (22:14) but there may be particular exceptions (22:15). We thus have the general law against stealing, the outworking of that law in particular cases, and

48

instances where there is a question of the interrelation of that law and another (e.g., the law against murder, 22:2, 3). Clearly we are not given the specific application of the law in every conceivable circumstance. What we are given is specifics in cases where there may be doubt as to the application of the general law. Even the general law is a specific expression of a more pervasive principle of biblical ethics: "love your neighbor as yourself" (Rom. 13:8-10).

There is no conflict between the general principle and the specific command. Obedience to specific commands fulfils the requirement to love one's neighbor and vice versa (Rom. 13:9, 10). The same close relationship between a broad principle of biblical ethics (conformity to God's holiness) and specific commands occurs in Leviticus 19.

When people make "completeness" their ideal they often conclude that only laws which deal with specifics of an individual situation have any validity. The general principles are neglected. Thus we find situations where the Pharisees developed an elaborate and specific legalistic system using tradition to supplement the "incomplete" Scriptures and ignoring or contradicting the general commands and principles of the law (Matt. 15:1-9; 23:13-28).

The same error is in operation when men reject the specifics of Scripture as authority and appeal only to some extremely vague general principle which is made so general and abstract as to have no real practical relevance. Each approach fails to see the close interaction and relationship between general and particular in the Scriptures. So close is this relationship that we may proceed from specific application back to the general command and thus to other specific applications of that same general principle. Note how Paul applies the command that the ox that treads out the corn is allowed to eat of the grain (I Cor. 9:9-11; I Tim. 5:17, 18). He points out that God is not merely concerned with oxen. Rather the specific law applied to oxen is an expression of the more general principle that the workman should partake in the fruits of his labors. The same principle has other practical applications such as the support of those who labor in the gospel. (See appendix II for a consideration of some related questions.)

There are cases in which a general priniciple or teaching in Scripture is connected to one specific example or outworking of that principle. For example, when Jesus declared all foods clean (Mark 7:1-19), he was dealing with a specific error, that of the Pharisees. Yet the general declaration that all foods are clean is not to be restricted to that particular case. It is often argued that a belief in the sufficiency and sole authority of Scripture will leave us in the dilemma of the group who refused to eat potatoes because they were not mentioned in the Bible. That is not so. The problem in that case was requiring that the Bible give specific applications for every occasion rather than just general principles. Certainly the declaration of Jesus that all foods are clean covers this problem.

Whereas this point will generally be granted when it comes to ethical matters, it is often denied when it comes to the teachings of Scripture which bear on the classroom. We are taught that man is responsible to recognize and give thanks to the Creator whose power and deity is displayed by creation (Rom. 1:18-25). In the context Paul is particularly concerned with idolatry. Does that mean that the scientist who wants to view creation as an atheist or agnostic is not also condemned? He too does not recognize the power and deity of God displayed in the things he has made. Yet it will be argued by some that science *as* science or the scientist *as* scientist is not expected to recognize God. The defense of this position is that Paul is speaking against pagan idolaters not against atheistic scientists. The mentality of those who take this position is the same as the mentality of those who abstain from potatoes. They do not accept the fact that there are general principles as well as specific applications in Scripture. (See appendix III for further discussion.)

Thus the study of Scripture in order to see how it applies in the classroom is not just a search for vague principles or just a concentration on a few specifics such as evolution in science and pornography in literature. The principles of Scripture have many specific applications and the specific rules of Scripture lead us to general teachings which have more applications.

6. Humanist Expectations of Scripture

We have seen that the humanist attitude which makes completeness the standard of truth leads to problems with the Scriptures. According to such a view, unless Scripture contains every last detail, it is rejected as a standard. There are also problems relating to the subject matter. There are certain areas where the humanist has to have more information than the Bible supplies. When he rejects the Creator, he must substitute a speculative theory of origins. The key question becomes for him the question of how things came to be. And so he produces his evolutionary thesis which is one of growth from the simple to the complex. Hence he wants detailed information on the simple building blocks and the way they gradually united together to develop into the world.

When we approach the Scripture with these expectations, we find that it lacks vital information. It tells us that God created and hence does not give us a mechanical theory of origins. The humanist must reject Genesis 1 as a true or adequate description because it does not contain enough mechanical details. When Christians call Genesis 1 "poetic" and hence irrelevant to "science," they are actually saying that they have humanist expectations of the shape of real scientific knowledge.

Another example would be the history of animal husbandry. The Bible gives us some brief information of this question (Gen. 4:20). Against the background of the created relative positions of man and animals (Gen. 1:26) it is not particularly problematic that man should be a herder. What will be a problem will be ensuring that that relationship is properly maintained. Whether the ox should be muzzled is a legitimate and serious question in a structure which assumes

51

creation. The humanist cannot assume creation and created relationships. For him discussions about muzzles for oxen will seem unimportant, trivial and folksy.

Similarly the later biblical teaching presupposes the fact of providence. The fact that men are threshing is not itself problematic. In a world in which God in his long-suffering maintains sowing and harvest (Gen. 8:22) that is to be expected. The way man threshes must be ordered by the law of God but God did not need to give man, at the time of Moses, the specific command to thresh grain. The humanist, with his expectations as to the standard of truth and the importance of evolutionary origins, will see things differently. He will demand that the Bible, if it is to be the rule for agriculture, must contain detailed descriptions of the origins of, and the mechanics of, threshing.

7. The Interrelation of Biblical Truth

By way of summary we may say that there can be no playing off of general principles against specific teachings. We constantly seek to apply the Scripture and we constantly seek to understand the connection of the specific applications in the Scripture to the whole system of biblical truth. And this is hard work. There is no instantaneous academic and intellectual sanctification. There is no philosophical system that includes all that the Christian teacher needs to know. It is a matter of deeper growth into the fulness of biblical revelation.

Furthermore, true knowledge is bound up with obedience. We have no Christian academic system which we can hand to teachers regardless of their desire to do the truth. This does not mean that the Scripture does not say many concrete and specific things. It says more than enough, but are we ready to accept what it says when it goes counter to what we have believed and done? It is not a question of mere intellectual insight. It is a question also of the pride, stubbornness and depravity of the human heart.

Our incentive is the fact that Christ "became to us wisdom

from God, and righteousness and sanctification and redemption" in order that our confidence and boast may be in the Lord and not our own intellectual powers and insight (I Cor. 1:30, 31). Therefore we persevere, knowing that in his light we shall see light (Ps. 36:9).

Man's Knowledge of Creation

1. God's Answer to Job

We tend to see the Book of Job as concerned with the physical problem of suffering. Yet Job and his friends saw that much greater questions were involved. God's government of the creation, and man's ability to understand the ways of God were also at issue. In his answer God speaks to these points.

God calls to account man's ability to question the ways of God. Job lacks the power to rule the creation; he is ignorant. Job is questioned as to his knowledge and control of specific events. Is Job omniscient? "Do you know the time the mountain goats give birth? Do you observe the calving of the deer?" (39:1). Does Job's knowledge rule the creation?

> Is it by your understanding that the hawk soars,
> Stretching his wings toward the south?
> Is it at your command that the eagle mounts up
> And makes his nest on high? (39:26, 27)

God's questions concern the stars as well as the animal creation. "Do you know the ordinances of the heavens, or fix their rule over the earth?"

Of course all these questions require a negative answer. God alone is the Lord and all creatures are his servants. They obey his commands. The same understanding of the relation between God and creation is present in Jeremiah 31:35:

> Thus says the Lord,
> Who gives the sun for light by day,

53

And the ordinances of the moon and stars for light
by night.

In a related passage God speaks of his covenant with the day
and night (Jer. 33:20). The whole language of this relationship is the language of a covenant. God, the Lord, rules his
servant creation by commands and ordinances just as he rules
his servant Israel (e.g., Lev. 18:4; Ps. 99:7).

Job does not give the commands that God gives to creation
nor does he know them. The law by which God rules his
creation is not known to man.

2. Law in Mechanistic Science

It may come as a surprise that man does not know the
commands which God gives his created servants. There is a
common practice of equating certain human attempts to
describe the motion of the heavenly bodies with the "law of
God." As a matter of fact there is no biblical teaching which
indicates that, aside from the laws addressed specifically to
man, man may know God's commands to his creation.

Often it is claimed that we may appeal to the "law of
God" in creation as a source of information alongside of and
often in opposition to Scripture. This claim has no basis.
Certainly creation does tell man something, but what it
reveals is God's character, not the law by which God governs
creation. From the creation we see the power, majesty, and
divinity of the God who made all things (Ps. 19; Rom. 1:20).
We misunderstand "general revelation" if we direct our attention to human formulations rather than to the majesty of
God.

These supposed "laws" have often been thought to give a
complete understanding of the universe. They have been
formulated by men as part of the attempt at comprehensive
and exhaustive knowledge. A good example would be systems allied to Laplacian physics. According to these systems,
the universe consists of matter in motion in a fixed container
of space and time. This motion is ruled by mechanical laws.
Thus the system is termed "mechanistic." In such a system

the motion of any particle is determined by the prior motions of it and other particles. Man and all that he thinks and does is caught within the same system because man is an accumulation of particles. God is effectively shut out of the system. And many see these laws of physics as being God's laws, and believe that he will certainly not intervene to change or break his own laws. The laws become a barrier effectively shutting God out of his creation. God is lost behind a wall of impersonal mechanical law. At the most he can be the god who makes the mechanism at the beginning and then leaves it completely alone to operate according to the inbuilt forces. Any action by God on a particular part of creation is excluded. Thus there cannot be a miracle or providence. Prayer has no meaning since everything is determined by the way the mechanism was set at the beginning. Regeneration cannot be the mysterious work of the Holy Spirit but becomes the outworking of immanent forces.

3. God's Commands to the Creation

The Scripture does not see God as barred from creation by his law. He personally addresses his covenant servants. God commands his servants and they obey him (Gen. 1:14-18; Job 30:8-12, 34, 35; Ps. 104:5-9; Jer. 31:35-37; 33:19; Matt. 8:5-13). Thus God is free to change the usual orders that he gives to his servants (Josh. 10:12-14).

Scripture does allow us to say certain things about the commands which God addresses to the creation. They result in a certain regularity. Thus the result of God's covenant with day and night is that day and night have an appointed time (Jer. 33:20). God in mercy promises the regularity of days and seasons in order that man may continue to live upon the earth (Gen. 8:21, 22). Such is the regularity of the heavenly bodies that they determine seasons and years (Gen. 1:14). Thus we may say that God's commands ensure a regularity and dependability in the world. This is part of his mercy to man, for without that regularity human life would be impossible.

It may be objected that this contradicts what was said

above about the mysterious nature of God's ordinances. If they are regular, how can they be mysterious? This problem can be easily answered by pointing out that the regularity that we see is the *result* of commands which continue to remain mysterious to us. The motion of planets may approximate Kepler's laws of planetary motion but that does not prove that God speaks the language of Kepler!

When man sets himself up as God, he tries to pretend that he can understand all of creation. His knowledge has to be as broad as God's. In order to do this he has to simplify the world. He has to fit it into his intellectual structures. If there are remnants of mystery, then man's attempts to play God will have failed. Hence the possibility of mystery is denied. It is argued that any remnant of mystery destroys the possibility of true knowledge. In a sense that is true within the man-centered humanist system. He wants to be either God or nothing. He operates with the logical poles of total knowledge or total ignorance. On such a system it makes no sense to say that the ways of God are regular yet mysterious.

For the Christian this does make sense. We may do our work depending on the regularity of creation which God maintains in his providence. Our scientific formulations are only possible because there is that regularity. However we do not pretend that these formulations are comprehensive or formulate God's laws.

4. Atomism as an Illustration

The humanist faces a great problem as he tries to reduce the complexity of God's creation to simple laws which he can understand. There are always exceptions to his laws. The motions of the planets do not quite correspond to his theoretical "laws." Here is an element of mystery which threatens his pretense to understand comprehensively the universe. So the day is saved by a hypothesis. It is asserted that the motions of the smallest particles are absolutely regular and understandable. What causes the irregularities is the way these most elementary motions are combined

56

together. Hence the belief in atomism and the search for the ultimate simple particle. To avoid confusion in terminology it should be pointed out that the search today is being directed to sub-atomic particles, forces and fields; the "atom" having proved far from regular and simple.

"Atomism" is not restricted to physics. In many other fields there is an attempt to find simple and comprehensible units in order to overcome the complexity of God's creation. These attempts will appear successful because there is a regularity to God's creation on *every* level. Yet the humanist faces the same problems on the "atomic" level as any other level. There is not the simple, totally comprehensible order that his faith demands. Hence he may swing to the opposite pole and deny the existence of any regularity, and hence of any human knowledge of the universe.

5. "Theoretical" Language as an Illustration

If we think that there is a human intellectual system comprehending all of reality, then the "scientific" language of that system will have a greater claim to truth and accuracy than any other type of language. If we believe that the irregularities we observe in the everyday world can be reduced to the regular motion of atoms, then mathematical language about atomic motions will be seen as having exactness and accuracy as compared with "everyday" language. If there are no such comprehensive systems, then the contrast of "scientific" and "everyday" language loses its point. Thus to dismiss the Bible as written in "everyday, naive" language as opposed to "scientific, theoretical" language, assumes a very important point with which we must take issue.

6. Consequences of the Biblical Position

Knowing the limitations of our knowledge produces humility and yet a firm trust. We know that day and night, summer and winter, cold and heat continue, not because they are rooted in an impersonal law order but because a gracious and sovereign God so commands. We must also be aware of

57

the tendency to simplify the creation in order to fit it into an order that man can understand. We need to emphasize the limitations of human systems of classification and description.

This view destroys the possibility of building great, all-comprehensive intellectual systems. It emphasizes the partial nature of all human thought. It will therefore be rejected by those who want to think themselves capable of categorizing everything in their human system.

The consequence of creating an impersonal order of law is that this shields man from direct contact with the holy God. Sinful man desires such a shield. There are spiritual consequences of thinking this way for a believer. The final judgment being a direct act of God, becomes a remote possibility virtually excluded by the tendencies of the mechanistic system. Furthermore prayer loses meaning. So this is no mere intellectual question. Do we really want to live in the *presence* of a holy God?

7. God Ordains Whatever Comes to Pass and Man Is Responsible

For Scripture there is no contradiction between God's foreordination of all things and man's responsibility for his actions. This emerges clearly in what is both the central event in God's plan for human redemption and the great crime of human history: "this man, delivered up by the predetermined plan and foreknowledge of God, you nailed to a cross by the hands of godless men and put him to death" (Acts 2:23). God works all things according to the counsel of his will (Eph. 1:11) yet man is responsible for all his actions and will answer for them on the day of judgment (II Cor. 5:10, Eccles. 12:14; Matt. 12:36).

Therefore Scripture excludes any manner of thinking which would remove either God's sovereignty or human responsibility. In particular we may not say that circumstances force a man to act contrary to the law of God (James

1:14). Human actions are not explained merely from the forces and pressures brought to bear upon an individual. Situations may explain the context in which he acted; they do not explain the act.

The Humanist Position

As has been pointed out above, the humanist attempts to comprehend everything within his own system. In such a system man is a part of the great mechanism and has no freedom or moral responsibility. His atoms obey the same laws as all the other atoms. History written from this perspective will see human action as only the result of determining circumstances. Man is a pawn. Furthermore, this sort of history strives after the ideal of a comprehensive picture. The ideal history is one in which the interaction of all of the events and forces has been reduced to a mechanical model with man as just one more cog. Of course man would have to be God to be able to make such a picture. Since man however is not God, he is forced to simplify the situation arbitrarily. For example, economic "forces" or "class struggles" are used as simplifying factors. Even though the existence of some of these entities may be quite unproven, they still serve to give the illusion that the situation has been reduced to its elements.

For the person who thinks this way, certain aspects of biblical historiography pose problems. First, he finds separate accounts of the one event or series of events with no apparent concern to integrate them. The humanist cannot imagine any other way of writing history than the way he does it. He attempts to integrate all in a comprehensive picture. Where the Bible writers do not do this he assumes that there must have been separate authors: thus the so called "two accounts of creation" (Gen. 1:1—2:3 and 2:4—3:24). However there is nothing at all wrong with a separate analysis of factors in a situation. If one's ideal ceases to be the mechanical model of the event in which the relation of one factor to another is exhaustively known, then such separate analysis is quite proper. This is not to say that some integration of the events is in itself wrong. The author of Psalm 104 integrated elements from Genesis 2 into the chronological order of events of Genesis 1.

Christian History Writing

We must always recognize the partial nature of our analysis. We do not see the full picture. That does not mean that any history we do will be false. One can say something without saying, or pretending to say, everything. Further we do not seek to dissolve the actions and motives of individuals into amorphous, impersonal tendencies and forces. In Scripture individuals are significant because they are responsible creatures before God.

Educational Theory

It is not just in our view of history that belief in human responsibility is important. Much of psychology and related educational theory denies the reality of human responsibility. Man is seen as a conditionable blob of protoplasm.

Another version of the denial of human responsibility occurs in popular romanticism. The child is assumed to be basically good. Any evil he does is not his fault but due to the influences and restrictions of adults. The aim of education is then seen as removing obstacles to the child's natural desires to learn. Given complete freedom he will learn. Scripture rejects this, pointing out the foolishness and depravity of the child (Ps. 51:5; Prov. 22:15).

We cannot affirm that man is responsible in the subject matter of history and yet deny it in our educational theory and method.

8. The "Scientific" Significance of Prayer

It has been pointed out that a mechanistic view of law makes prayer meaningless, for according to it God cannot break his "laws" to answer prayer. The truth is that the biblical teaching about prayer should surely lead Christians to question the mechanistic philosophy. Our sovereign God is not lost behind a wall of impersonal mechanical law, but is personally present to act on a particular part of his creation in answer to prayers of responsible men. Sadly many believers have taken refuge in dualism and have tried to keep their prayer and science separate. Rejecting this solution we are made to realize that *there must be something wrong with the mechanistic view.* Thus what the Bible says about prayer is not to be relegated to a "religious" category. The biblical doctrine of prayer is of great significance for science.

This section could even have begun with biblical teaching on prayer rather than God's answer to Job. The same conclusions would have been reached. Scripture is a unity. There is no one passage with which we must start in order to reach a certain conclusion. There are many roads to the same conclusion.

The Sobriety of the Christian Life

Under this heading I would like to explore the implications of the deep, steadfast, moral earnestness which characterizes the walk of faith. "Sobriety" or "sober-mindedness" may not be the word to include all of these ideas but it excludes any frivolous, sporadic application of biblical truth. The believer is to "be steadfast, immovable, always abounding in the work of the Lord" (I Cor. 15:58). He is to do everything to the glory of God (I Cor. 10:31). He is to abstain from every form of evil (I Thess. 5:22). All of his speech must be edifying; none of it may be foolish and coarse (Eph. 4:29; 5:3, 4). There are no intervals in this walk. The believer cannot suspend his godliness. It is to be his constant characteristic. His attitude to the perversions of the ungodly is not a detached, clinical professionalism but a moral abhorrence (Eph. 5:5-20).

1. Teaching Literature

These considerations are of crucial importance to our approach to literature. Drama forms a clear example. Can a believer play the role of a godless character? Can he, even as an actor, enter into that role and utter godless words with every appearance of sincerity that he can simulate? Certainly the Bible reports godless words, and a believer might be called upon to do so as a witness in court, but this is very different from a Christian entering into those words and attempting to convey them as plausible and earnest. To convey the words in this way a Christian must step outside of himself and his Christian earnestness.

A related question is that of whether we can read literature for "entertainment" and "relaxation." This is not necessarily a problem for the classroom but it is closely related to the problem of the weight that we give to literary ability in the assessment of a work. The problem can be put as follows. If we are entertained and impressed by godlessness depicted with skill and subtlety, what happens to our moral earnestness? Yet on the other hand, should we not appreciate a talent which is the gift of God however it may be misused? There is a danger, in this formulation of the problem; the danger of oversimplification. A talent, even if it be a gift of God, is not at the disposal of a sovereign individual who autonomously rules his own life. Refusal to acknowledge God leads to foolishness and corruption (Rom. 1:21-32). We cannot view literature as though it shows to us a pure God-given talent. It shows rather misuse, perversion, a decline into foolishness as men vaunt their own wisdom. Our assessment must be mixed with grief and concern. This is not to say that all non-Christian literature must display a gloomy pessimism. On the contrary, God's gifts may fill the unbeliever's heart with joy and gladness (Acts 14:17). Our sadness may stand in sharp contrast to the unbeliever's joy because we know that for him the end is weeping and gnashing of teeth. Our assessment must be characterized by concern that the unbeliever's joy is degenerating into frothy vanity and will end in misery.

Our assessment must also be characterized by grief that his seriousness and concern becomes hollow and pretentious. Our moral earnestness leads not to a self-righteous condemnation but to a real concern for men who go the way of destruction. Moreover, as a result of our assessment we have a righteous indignation that what God has given should be used to attack and blaspheme him. Yes, man does indeed receive the good gifts of God. But that makes him all the more liable to God, not less so. In our critique of literature we must see the corruption that is taking place—the perversion of what God gave.

The note of grief and concern is a good one to stress when we turn to the Christian production of literature. Too much "Christian literature" reflects a rosy picture of life even more simplistic than that of Job's comforters. Joy in the Lord must have, as a necessary corollary, grief and indignation over sinners. This does not mean that all Christian literature must take the literary form of a sermon. Sobriety determines the attitude of the author, not the literary form of the work.

This approach will cut across the modern emphasis on spontaneity. The moral earnestness of the believer is something that has to be striven for. It is a battle with himself as he seeks to subject himself to the law of God (I Cor. 9:24-27). It is not spontaneous and effortless. If one teaches the child to simply "express himself," then one teaches him to express corruption and depravity because that is what is in the child's heart (Ps. 51:5, Prov. 22:15). We may applaud the rejection of an artificial and contriving style, lacking in feeling and depth. But the positive answer is not to open the door to whatever may be in the depraved heart of man. The answer lies in training and discipline that is concerned for the heart as well as literary expression.

2. Teaching Mathematics

Another area in which moral earnestness raises questions is mathematics. Mathematics has been one of the disciplines most affected by rationalism. The simpler order, by which man could understand the complexities of the universe, was thought to be a mathematical one. While some still hold this, others have realized that Newton and La Place did not say the last word in physics. Physical reality has proven very difficult to reduce to one comprehensive mathematical system. This, plus the emergence of many different mathematical systems, has made many skeptical of whether there is a necessary connection between human mathematical systems and the structure of reality. Why then should we pursue mathematics? The answer often given is that mathematics is an interesting game. Much of it has no meaning or purpose but is fun to play the game. Thus there has been a swing from seeing mathematics as the revelation of the order of the universe to seeing it as having no real meaning and purpose. Our question is whether a Christian can view mathematics as just a meaningless purposeless game.

Our criterion for the usefulness of mathematics will be different from that of the unbeliever. For practical purposes the unbeliever may be ready to make use of mathematics which gives an approximation of the order of the universe, but his ideal is a mathematical system which perfectly comprehends that order. We, on the other hand, are content to use an approximation. The regularity which God maintains in the creation means that there are many rule-of-the-thumb approaches which we can use. Mathematics is not reduced to meaninglessness for us because it is imperfect.

There is an order, a logic, in mathematical systems only because God in mercy maintains the regularity of his creation (Gen. 8:22; II Peter 3:3-9). Mathematics bears testimony to the longsuffering of God in preserving the present heavens and earth until judgment day, and therefore requires that we give thanks to God. The Christian does not suspend his godliness, but lives in grateful moral earnestness (II Peter 3:11-14. 18, 19).

3. Teaching Art

The artist is often faced with the interaction of God and man in history. Too often we find the argument that the use

64

of decorative art for the tabernacle and the temple justifies any sort of art. However, when the artist attempts to depict an historical event, especially one from biblical history, he runs against the commandment forbidding pictures of God. Often this is by-passed with the claim that Scripture forbids only pictures of God which are worshiped. This attempt to evade the clear meaning of the commandment is refuted by Isaiah 40:12-26. One cannot represent God because there is no earthly image to which he may be likened: "To whom then will you liken God? Or what likeness will you compare with Him?" (v. 18). It is the character of God, not just the danger of idolatry, which lies behind the prohibition of images.

Western artists have offered several solutions to the problems of God's actions in history. Sometimes they have taken over the pagan notion of god as a mere superman and represented "God" as a big man. This is blasphemous. Or, again they have worked against the background which has seen God as excluded from the cosmos by his own laws. In that tradition the artist has been able to completely ignore God. He thinks he has shown the real factors in an historical situation when he shows the human actors. Hence such art exalts man.

Likewise art depicting Jesus has a number of special problems, but generally speaking it falls into the same two categories. The Scriptures are emphatic that Jesus was God who appeared in the flesh to eyewitnesses (I John 1:1-3; John 1:14). Jesus was not God hidden inside a human body. He was God and man, and to be able to represent him the artist would have to able to drag from his imagination an image which could display, not just any man, but the glory of God in the flesh. The pagan, effeminate, romantic images, which artists have produced of Jesus, are evidence of how impossible such a task is. One can also think of attempts to show the glory of the risen Lord. Do any have the effect upon us that the glorious Lord has (Rev. 1:17)? Of course not, for although a description of the glory of the Lord may be attempted, no human artist could possible capture it. On the other hand, Jesus in the state of his humiliation is depicted as a man. Where the Renaissance and Enlightenment glorification of man has been at work, Jesus is seen as the great man. Against this background it is easy to ignore the biblical emphasis that both deity and humanity occur together and are revealed by Jesus.

The problems raised here for art go far beyond merely "biblical" art to the depiction of any historical scene. How does the artist avoid either depicting God, whose decrees are indeed mysterious, or glorifying man by excluding God? At the present I do not know an answer to this question, and I suspect one might not be possible.

We find therefore that the Bible does allow decorative art, yet it forbids pictures of God. Clearly, then, we cannot view all of what we commonly call "art" as one. The reason we have problems in developing Christian critiques is that we often accept what our culture and its tradition present to us. We take "art" as "art" and then come to the conclusion, based on the prohibition of images, that all art is banned or to the contrary conclusion, based on temple decoration, that all art is permitted.

For instance, in which category do landscapes or portraits fall? Should we relate them to pictures of God and ban them or relate them to decorative art and permit them? Whatever the answer to this question, there is a danger in taking pictures of God and decorative art as fixed points to which all other art should be related. The situation may not be this simple. We should not make the mistake of ignoring the human heart.

One of the issues that has to be explored is the relationship between the artist and the craftsman. In our western tradition the artist has been seen almost universally as a man gifted with a certain mystical or prophetic insight. In the pagan background the gift comes from the gods. When the gods are removed and replaced by an ideal realm or a law order, the artist is one who has insight into this realm. The artist with this insight stands separate from the craftsman

66

who has merely skill or dexterity. Once the impersonal law order is removed the whole basis for the mystical "insight" collapses. Hence the questions we must ask about art are: does the artist see himself as a man with prophetic insight to lay bare a more ultimate order, an order which reduces the irregularity of appearance to an intellectual simplicity? Or does the artist see himself as a craftsman, skilled by God to shape forms, an activity which is reflective, imitative and derivative of the creative activity of God? The former conveys no idea of labor. The artist may meditate and pray for inspiration but it comes as a flash of insight because there is a simple order, totally comprehensible to the human mind, into which his mind enters. The craftsman must work. There are no simplifying intellectual short-cuts.

In the previous section it has been pointed out that the man who believes in comprehensive human knowledge (or rationalism) tends to simplify the world in order to understand it. These tendencies will also influence art. A clear example is the attempt in cubism to reduce reality to geometric shapes. The artist is influenced by the same tendencies when he attempts to capture the essence of a historical movement or event in one picture. It is at this point that a problem is created in that God's agency is excluded. Can there be "artists" without this "insight"? We come back to the problem of distinguishing "artist" and "craftsman."

Some may be concerned with the inconclusive nature of this discussion of art. Yet if we take the partial character of our knowledge and our spiritual ignorance seriously, we will meet this in many areas. None of us have all the answers.

How to Approach Further Explorations

The approach that has been used so far has been to consider certain biblical teachings and to suggest the implications of these teachings in various disciplines. An alternative approach would be to take the disciplines individually and to try to bring to bear all the biblical considerations relevant to that discipline. Such an approach certainly has its value. Indeed it has to be done at some stage. Nevertheless we need to be careful lest the division into disciplines imposes artificial constraints on our thought. We need to start with the Scriptures and to see where their teaching leads us. If we begin with the assumption of a set school curriculum we may create problems. For example, I believe that if we assume that uttering godless words in drama must be a part of the curriculum, because every school does it, then we will have to ignore or argue away certain emphases of Scripture. We may also make the mistake of expecting the biblical passages to correspond to our academic divisions. For example, take the biblical teaching that in all he does the believer must glorify God. Our academic categorization would tend to put that into "ethics." I have suggested that if we live out that teaching it will effect our approach to literature and mathematics.

Divisions into subject areas tend to be intellectual divisions of the subject matter. There are broad issues of approach which cross such divisions. Furthermore our growth in thinking correctly in these areas cannot be divorced from our sanctification. If Christ is not divided into intellectual and practical halves, then our growth into his likeness should not be so divided. It is as we grow as believers that this growth shows in our teaching and study. If we are engaged in a particular discipline, that growth should show in our particular area. We should recognize that each man has his gift from God, therefore we cannot say that our growth in any aspect of our obedience to our Lord is strictly proportional to growth in the other areas. Nevertheless, to use a figure, we should not expect to progress 95 percent of the way in Christian mathematics and only 5 percent in loving our brethren.

There is, for instance, no one final finished "Christian" mathematics. That is a kind of intellectual perfectionism into which we shall fall if we believe that reality may be reduced to one simple system. Rather there will be mathematics that will be more or less Christian. While we may heartily welcome a Christian textbook in which progress has been made towards the goal, we must stress the personal attitude of the teacher. A teacher who wants to hold on to rationalism and intellectual pride would counteract such a textbook.

Whoever agrees with any idea presented here, may justly ask how he is to make further progress in the directions suggested. To begin with, it seems to me that an essential aspect of progress is an attitude of detachment from this world and its intellectual and educational fads. If the believer is required to test all things (I Thess. 5:21), then he cannot assume their truth. He must ask the reason and basis for a belief no matter how widely assumed it is. Anything less is conformity to this world. At the same time he must be alert to passages of Scripture which others have ignored, glossed over, or relegated to the "non-scientific" category.

Our great practical problem is that we cannot imagine any other way of doing and thinking than the one which has become accepted in our culture. We do not question "self-evident" truths. To make progress we must be especially sensitive to passages in which the Scriptures appear to be taking a different approach to the one we normally take. Often this will stimulate us to reexamine accepted dogma.

A study of the history of ideas is also valuable. Certain ideas have become so familiar that we have lost sight of their philosophical and spiritual roots. Another approach is to look at the arguments or "facts" put forward to support positions which Scripture tells us are wrong. Examining the way the evidence has been interpreted may throw light on the false assumptions involved in that system.

1. Teaching Botanical Classification

Why do we accept a classification system based largely upon the seed leaves and flowering parts of plants? The answer to the question is complex. In part, the answer will reflect the influence of non-Christian thought upon biology, especially the philosophy of Plato. Modern botanical classification begins in an atmosphere of Christianized Platonism, concluding that every biological group must be clearly transparent and distinct. Platonism tries to resolve the problem of the complexity and the order of the universe by assigning the order to fixed eternal ideas or structures which are imposed upon a material which was without order or form. Thus we have an imposed structure opening the way to a true and complete knowledge of the universe by knowledge of the ideas. When non-Christian Platonism is fused with Christianity, "God" is regarded as having created the ideas separate from the material. Hence the "Christian" Platonist interprets Adam's naming of the animals as indication that Adam recognized the eternal idea which gave that animal group its distinctive nature. "Naming the animals" thus becomes the responsibility to recognize the clear and distinct forms of the animal world.

As a result the Platonist is forced to look for some stable and fixed factor which will give him the clue to recognizing the different animal and plant groups. Thus a Platonist botanist like John Ray in the seventeenth century rejected systems of classification based upon changeable characteristics like height and medicinal use, in favor of a "natural" system based on more fixed characteristics like seedleaves, flowers, etc. The fixity and order revealed by this classification system then becomes the proof for the existence of the god who made the ideas.

The problem, as the Christian would expect, was that it proved impossible to carry through the "natural" system. Some plants simply cannot be classified by the criteria used for most other plants. Hence the groupings gained by this system look very artificial and contrived because they have been based upon but a few characteristics.

The failures of the whole system prepare for the theory of evolution. Sadly by the nineteenth century this Platonic theory of classification had been confused with the biblical doctrine of creation in distinct kinds. It was realized that there were cases in which it was very difficult to divide animals or plants into their "kinds." Therefore it seemed that the biblical doctrine of creation had been disproved. In reality it was merely the Platonic doctrine that was in trouble. The Bible does not guarantee, especially in the light of man's partial knowledge of the creation and in the light of a fallen world, that the different kinds will be instantly recognizable and classifiable by man. However, with non-Christian philosophy dominating Christian thinking, the discovery of difficulties was seen as a blow to Christianity. There was a swing to the opposite extreme, to evolution, and thus to a denial of the reality of any of the distinctions and characteristics of biological groups which are clear to the eye. This swing is characteristic of the tendency of non-Christian thought to move from the view that every biological group must be clearly and transparently distinct (Platonism) to the denial of the reality of divisions clearly visible (evolution); this is to say there was a swing from rationalism to irrationalism. The Christian does not have this problem. He can recognize the order present in the biological world, and yet he does not assume that every division will be clearly evident to him. He knows that God created in distinct kinds, not because his rationality can prove it exhaustively, but because God tells him so.

A Christian could come to these conclusions in many different ways. For example he could, as a teacher of biology who is required to test all things, question the commonly received system of classification. What right does it have to be regarded as the only system? Could other systems have a validity? Alternatively, in studying the history of biology he might recognize the clear Platonic influences at work in Ray and his successors. As a different approach he could study the significance of I Kings 4:33, which indicates a sort of classification of trees based on size. But sometimes this passage is quoted as an example of the "unscientific" approach of the Bible. The alert Christian, however, will ask why systems based upon something other than size have the claim to greater scientific rigor and respectability. If he does, he will soon discover that such a claim presupposes a rationalistic simplification of the plant creation. He will discover that the order and diversity of the plant creation cannot be subsumed under one classification system based on one set of criteria. He might also come to these same conclusions by considering the arguments commonly presented to defend evolutionary theory.

2. Teaching "New Math"

The Christian who is required to test all things will not be satisfied with traditional mathematics purely because it is traditional. Nor will he embrace the new math merely to show that he is progressive. The Christian will be concerned that many curricula, hailed as new and better, seem to produce pupils who cannot make use of the simplest practical mathematics. When one studies the rationale given for new programs in math, it is easy to see how a situation like this can arise.

The thesis is that if we show the child the logical structure and reasoning behind simple mathematical operations, this will enable him to understand and do mathematics much better than if he merely learns by rote. The problem with this is not the idea that understanding promotes learning. The problem is the assumption of a logical system which supposedly lies behind simple arithmetic. One quickly recognizes the rationalistic assumptions. Arithmetic is to be reduced to a simpler, but more abstract logical order. Since this is the logical basis of arithmetic, one does not really need to learn arithmetical operations. Once one sees the logical basis one can always understand how to do the arithmetic required.

The supposed logical base may be more abstract but is it really the rational basis of mathematics? Certainly, as would be expected in a world in which God preserves order, relationships between different branches of mathematics are

72

evident. Nevertheless, as the paradoxes of set theory demonstrate, there have been tremendous problems in the way of this supposedly logical system. In practice the child may simply be confronted with a set of abstract terminology and learn nothing. What the rationalist sees as the logical key to mathematics becomes, like all rationalist systems, merely proof that academics can say simple things in obscure ways.

The mathematics out of which these new curricula have grown has raised fundamental problems about the nature and validity of human knowledge. What is the relationship between the existence of three cats in a room and my abstract concept "three"? The commonly used "experimental" or "laboratory" approach to elementary mathematics grows out of a certain philosophical answer to these problems. When we count "one, two, three cats" and "one, two, three dogs" we are taking an abstract number and seeing it as applicable to different situations. How do you prove that is valid? The Christian has no problem because there is a God-created regularity in the cosmos and he can always appeal to the use of numbers in the Bible. The unbeliever has no such basis of appeal. What he may try to do is to show that "one-, two-, threeness" exists in the structure of things. The child is not to be taught to count "one, two, three" by some authority which could be right or wrong but to see intuitively that this is part of the structure of reality.

Of course this approach goes hand in hand with the contemporary contempt of authority and memorization. We would not deny that one remembers very well the things he learns for himself. Nevertheless it is clearly evident from Scripture, especially in the Book of Proverbs, that one should heed instruction so as to avoid the long and painful process of learning by experience! In practice, especially when left to themselves, only a few students make the required "discoveries." Those who do not grasp the abstract concepts required of them are left without either understanding or practical knowledge based on rote memorization. There is a tendency to look upon such students as simply "poorer

73

students." Rationalism gives preference to students able to understand its abstract formulations. It thus creates a social distinction between workers and academics to correspond with the distinction between the complexities of the experienced world and its (supposedly) underlying logical order. The Christian must not make this distinction. For him the theoretical mathematician is not dependent upon a different sort of an order than that of the shop assistant counting change according to a memorized system.

To recapitulate, this section began with the problem that some students are being left without a practical knowledge of mathematics. A Christian will react to that problem. Often he will do so more readily than the non-Christian because he has a great distrust of human methods, however "new" and "modern." He will also do so because he does not make a sharp distinction between academic and non-academic students. Finally, the Christian will recognize a complex rationalistic abstraction to be pretension rather than the only true basis upon which mathematics can be built. The next step is one which I feel should be made but which is beyond my competence. We need a Christian analysis of set theory and the related question of transfinite numbers. The rationalistic mathematician would be appalled that I have dared to criticize modern mathematical education without an exhaustive understanding of modern mathematics. My answer would be that the Bible recommends that we judge the tree by its fruit. Where the result has been an abstract rationalism in mathematical education, we do well to look for evidence of rationalism in the basic theory. Certainly we need the collaboration of Christian mathematicians, but the Christian teacher must not be overawed by the "experts." He has a right to question the system, or bad parts of it, if the fruit is rotten.

There is no one way that we recognize errors in our teaching. The concern that the practical teacher has for whether the pupil learns or not is a major source of stimulus and insight. The unbeliever will be awed by the "expert" educationalists who decree from their academic heights the methods which must be followed. If we do not allow the existence of some distinct abstract "laws of education," then we will test the experts by the rule that is in the hand of every teacher: the Scriptures. Our problem has been our acceptance of methods and ideas which we may not have agreed with or even understood. We accepted them because we did not know of a better way. We suppressed our sense that they did not fit certain aspects of biblical teaching. The need is to go back to the Scriptures and develop a truly critical Christian attitude. Then Christian teachers will be fulfilling their purpose in our Christian schools.

Appendix I to Chapter 3
Social Structure in the New Testament

A common example raised in this discussion is the position of women in the New Testament church. It is claimed that the rules of Paul in I Corinthians 14 and I Timothy are directed to the particular cultural circumstances and do not apply in today's different social and cultural setting. This is then advanced as an example of the law of God being changed by changes in culture and social structure.

If one goes by what the biblical text itself says, then this explanation can be summarily dismissed. Paul does not appeal to the customs of the time. He appeals to the created order when he talks about the position of women (see I Cor. 11:3, 7-9; I Tim. 2:13, 14). There is no proof for the common belief that Paul's instructions concerning the behavior of women in worship reflected a local custom of women covering their heads or veiling their faces as a sign of modesty. Certainly Paul appeals to "nature" in I Corinthians 11:14 but a simple check of the use of "nature" by Paul shows that he means the created order rather than mere contemporary custom.

There is thus nothing in the texts involved to indicate that the New Testament teaching on social roles was a mere concession to the times. Rather it is based on the order of creation.

Appendix II to Chapter 3
The "Letter" of the Law

The teaching of the New Testament has been interpreted as an aversion to any concern with the details of the law. Any interest in the detailed outworking of the law is condemned as Pharisaism or legalism.

The problem with this interpretation is that it makes Paul a legalist. The same Paul who says that the letter kills can appeal to a law about oxen. We must not confuse the law as a way of obtaining salvation with the law as a guide for life. Rigorous adherence to the details of the law will not save a man. Yet the saved man who lives by the Spirit is to fulfill what the law demands.

A clear proof that concern for the law is not forbidden in the New Testament is Matthew 23:23. The Pharisees are condemned for losing sight of the great principles of the law in their concern for its detailed ourworking. Jesus does not say that they should have abandoned the command to tithe in order to concentrate on justice, mercy and faithfulness. On the contrary he says "these are the things you should have done without neglecting the others."

In the passage where Paul contrasts the "letter" and the "Spirit" (II Cor. 3:4-18) he is not making a contrast between the detailed rules of the law and the essence of the law. It is not a keeping of the "spirit" of the law that gives life. That is still legalism. Paul's contrast is between the letters of the law on stone and the work of the Spirit of Christ on the heart. The external letters written on stone have no power to change the heart and so bring only condemnation to transgressors. It is the Spirit writing "on tablets of human hearts" that gives life. The very fact that the law works condemnation is evidence of its dignity. It does this because it is

God's law that is broken. Hence the respect that the New Testament grants the law as a guide for our conduct as believers.

Appendix III to Chapter 3
General and Particular

It may be objected that to talk of "general" and "particular" is to import a secular philosophical distinction into the Scriptures. Certainly the terms "general" and "particular" can be colored by their use in philosophical systems. That applies to many of the words we use and to many of the Greek words of the New Testament. The danger is not the use of words. It is importing along with those words connotations which distort the truth of the Scriptures we are trying to expound.

In Matthew 23:23 Jesus talks of the "weightier provisions of the law." In Romans 13:9 Paul says that all the commandments are summed up in the saying "You shall love your neighbor as yourself." It is this biblical distinction between the basic principles motivating the law and the individual expression of those principles which I seek to express by the distinction between "general" and "particular."

Apendix IV to Chapter 3
The Approach of the A.A.C.S.

Anyone familiar with the philosophy of the cosmonomic idea of Dooyeweerd and Vollenhoven and its extension and popularization, through the Association for the Advancement of Christian Scholarship, will note the obvious differences between this work and that approach. One of the great problems of that philosophy is the tendency to see the proof of its validity in its complexity and intellectual sophistication rather than in the agreement of its results and conclusions with the Scripture. In a day when many Christians are desperately searching for an alternative to the great secular

77

systems, the philosophy of the cosmonomic idea attracts by its apparent intellectual completeness and sophistication. Here is a worthy rival of the non-Christian systems. Yet there lies the problem. Have we accepted the non-Christians' test of truth?

Its view of organic development in history is where a clear conflict occurs between the philosophy and the Bible. This is a crucial point for the Christian school movement as the argument that the school is a sphere separate from the home depends upon the theory that the organic development of society causes a differentiation of school from home. This organic differentiation is thus in effect a cultural change which changes the law of God, in this case removing control of education from the control of parents.

The proponents of the AACS philosophy will object that I have treated the Bible as a "textbook" of history and extracted from it a philosophical theory of history which it was not designed to teach. What is said in the first two sections about the Bible as a "textbook" is relevant to this question but there are also other considerations. Can we know before we examine the Bible what it may or may not teach? Does the Bible tell us that we should not use its words and teaching to test philosophical systems? The restrictions that the philosophy makes upon the use of the Bible are imposed from without on philosophical considerations. Thus biblical authority has effectively been nullified.

It will be objected that every author, this one included, approaches the Bible with certain presuppositions and tends to impose these upon Scripture. That is certainly true. Scripture itself recognizes the blindness that keeps men from seeing the truth. But our blindness is all the more reason why we should not declare the words of Scripture as unable to judge our human philosophical system. It is all the more reason why we should not lay down rules for the way we may use Scripture without testing those rules against Scripture itself.

This problem emerges most clearly at the points where the philosophy appeals to Scripture. For example, it refers to

Scripture for the "creation, fall, redemption motive" and for "out of the heart are the issues of life." Can we go back to Scripture to see whether ideas and words have been wrenched from their contexts and subjected to philosophical allegorization? Surely the danger of "proof-texting" must be greater in a system which forbids the careful testing of its philosophical premises by the words of Scripture.

It may be objected that this approach imposes upon the individual disciplines the tyranny of the theologian and of "biblicism." However the real problem of tyranny is the tyranny of the philosophical system over the individual disciplines. My own professional calling is that of a historian. If I am required to interpret history in terms of "organic differentiation," then the philosophy is imposing its tyranny upon me. Of course, as an historian, I am aware of the development of the organic model of historical development in non-Christian philosophical systems. I am aware of the way that the popular notions of "progress" and "development" have distorted our understanding of history and made even Christians susceptible to reading history in these terms. I am familiar with the allegorical exegesis of Genesis 2:15 which takes the command to cultivate the garden as a command to develop all the potentialities which God had built into the creation. Yet as a Christian historian I cannot allow myself to be dominated by popular non-Christian ideas. I must not distort the material to fit into the current fads in thought. To read history in terms of organic differentiation is to impose a distortion upon the evidence. I am perturbed by people who confidently declare that the separation of the school from the home is a product of the modern differentiation of society and was unknown in biblical times. Am I to suppress my historical knowledge at this point? In theory the philosophy is supposed to be subject to refinement and criticism from those in specific disciplines. But can the philosophy of the cosmonomic idea survive the rejection of its basic thesis of historical development?

I am not claiming that the historian should be free to

approach the "neutral facts" with an "open" mind. He will be under some authority which supplies his perspectives and tells him what tests to apply in order to distingush truth from error in his field. To be under the authority of the words of God given in Scripture is not to be under an alien tyranny. To be subject to a human philosophical system is to be under tyranny.

Chapter 4
WORLD
The Purpose of a Christian School Is . . .

*That the World Might See the Willingness of Teacher,
Parent, Church, and Pupil to Deny Satan and Self
and Take Up Our Cross to Follow Christ*

LEONARD J. COPPES*

Why should we have a Christian school? This question is
being asked by more and more Christians today. Some evan-
gelicals are driven to start schools because of the rather spec-
tacular gains of atheistic secularism which is beginning to
dominate the public school system. The Protestant commitment to education, however, has a much longer history,
dating from Zwingli's and Calvin's emphasis on the importance of the ability of every Christian to read the Bible for
himself. Children and adults were taught to read for this
purpose. The American scene ultimately produced a general
concern for education and the great majority of the American Protestant community became satisfied to allow the state
to take over education. This satisfaction with state run education developed slowly from the time of the founding of the
Americas to the beginnings of the twentieth century. It

---

*Dr. Leonard Coppes is the pastor of Calvary Orthodox Presbyterian Church in
Harrisville, Pennsylvania. Since coming to Harrisville in 1971, he has provided
active leadership in the fledgling Christian school which is now in existence there.
Dr. Coppes' publications include Bible studies in Mark and Romans, and *Whatever Happened to Biblical Tongues?*

81

involved ignoring or denying important aspects of the Christian faith, especially that true wisdom and knowledge are in Christ, from God, and revealed in the Bible. At first, public education was staffed by a majority who accepted this important truth, but eventually the majority became the minority.

Today the assumption that Christians and non-Christians can cooperate in education is becoming more and more difficult to accept. If Christ is not clearly acknowledged as Lord, he becomes the object of ignorance and ridicule. Public schools have denied basic biblical truths such as creation, Christian morality, man's responsibility to be God's servant, discipline (controlled force rather than violence as a necessary instrument to control and punish wrongdoing), etc.

We Christians ought to establish a clear witness regarding our understanding of and willingness to exhibit the biblical principle of denying Satan and self and taking up our cross to follow Christ in everything. Establishing Christian schools is a most desirable instrument both in training our children as to how they may thus please God and in showing the unbelieving world our unique and blessed service to our Lord.

Thus, we address ourselves to the proposition that one purpose of the Christian school is "that the world might see the willingness of teacher, parent, church and pupil to deny Satan and self and take up our cross to follow Christ in everything." Our treatment will begin by examining the biblical support for the premise that being a believer necessarily involves a willingness to deny oneself and to educate one's children even at the cost of self-denial. We will spend some time focusing on the objects of our witness and, in general, how that witness is directed toward them. We will review some of the ways this witness is expressed specifically in a Christian school. Our treatment will conclude with a discussion of the degree to which such a witness should be pursued.

You Should Be Willing to Make Sacrifices!

Does Christianity necessarily involve suffering? Does child-rearing necessarily involve self-sacrifice? Can we witness through the suffering which is involved in the self-sacrifice of child-rearing?

We believe that all of these questions can be answered with a loud "yes!"; the first and second because they are clearly stated in the Scriptures, and the last because it is inseparably related to the first two. In this section we will seek to show why it is that child-rearing and Christian obedience involve (1) self-denial and (2) educating our children in obedience to God's covenant with man.

1. Witness and Suffering

The theme "suffering for Christ" is often on the lips of Christians but seldom actually experienced. This is partly because, like the disciples, we conceive of Christianity as an earthly kingdom of splendor. Jesus patiently but pointedly taught his followers that following him is closely tied to obedience, appointment unto action, hatred by the present world order and those committed to it, and finally, to witness. As we will see, all of these are inseparably bound together.

The Unexpected Suffering

The Jews were expecting a messianic king (a Christ) to appear and lead them into victory over all their enemies. The disciples had been deeply influenced by this idea. At first they accepted Jesus as the great prophet, but slowly and with stumbling steps they came to realize that he was a great deal more than a prophet. In Mark 8:27 Jesus asked them who other men said he was. They gave several current explanations. Then he asked them what they thought. Here Jesus drew their understanding into an open confession, as is illustrated by Peter who responded, "Thou art the Christ."

What follows is most instructive in showing us what Peter and the others meant. Jesus immediately began to teach them about his suffering and death, stating this plainly (as

Mark records). The Jewish idea of the "Christ" was that he was to be a victorious military leader who would lead them to rule the world. This was far removed from any concept of the suffering servant. Without hesitation, Peter took Jesus aside and began privately to rebuke him. Peter was dumbfounded by what appeared to be an unexplainable contradiction in Jesus' teaching about his future. He looked forward to earthly glory, but Jesus wanted him (indeed, all of the twelve) to understand that his was a heavenly kingdom preceded by earthly suffering and self-sacrifice. Hence, Jesus did not let this matter remain private. He turned so he viewed the rest of the disciples and he rebuked Peter strongly, if not shockingly: "Get thee behind me, Satan; for thou mindest not the things of God, but the things of men." He perceived in Peter's words Satan's wiles. In the temptation, the Devil had offered Jesus alternate routes to kingly power. But Jesus knew that there was but one path to the kingdom. It lay through the agony of Calvary. It was no quickly conceived road, but was divinely set forth from eternity and divinely declared from before the creation (Eph. 1:4). Jesus, the Son of God, fixed himself on that path.

Jesus' path was but an example of that path which every true believer is to follow. Jesus summoned the multitude so all could hear what he was about to say (Mark 8:34). He set before them the by-word of discipleship. Following Jesus is something other than enjoying earthly glory and luxury. Indeed, it begins with self-denial. Certainly this is a major theme in Christ's ministry.

This is explained somewhat later (Mark 10:17-22) in the report about a rich young man who eagerly ran up to Jesus. Here was a zealous young man full of great expectations hoping to gain great insight from Jesus as to how he might inherit eternal life. Although he knelt showing his respect, he did not see that the path to eternal life was paved first by denying his own understanding of reality and replacing it with God's.

With masterful hand Jesus thrusts truth into the darkness of the man's soul. "One thing thou lackest." Jesus without invitation sought to fill this latter need. He told the man, "Go, sell whatsoever thou hast, and give to the poor, and thou shalt have treasure in heaven; and come, follow me."

The all-knowing Lord knew the extent of the man's wealth and his attachment to it. His love was for this world rather than for God. Jesus challenged him to re-align his priorities: "Come, follow me." The battle of the mind reveals itself to be a battle of the will. Self-denial reaches to one's concept of his earthly goods. As God, Jesus orders the man's submission. Those who seek eternal life thus jeopardize their worldly goods. All is payable upon God's demand. The attitude of willing submission must be absolute. The extent of compliance is defined by God's commands. Jesus demanded all so that his self-indulgence (v. 22) could be exposed. So with us; if eternal life is our goal or possession it means a willingness to render all our worldly goods, if necessary, to meet the Lord's demands. The battle of the will is shown to be a battle of the soul

> For whosoever would save his life shall lose it;
> and whosoever shall lose his life for my sake and
> the gospel's shall save it (Mark 8:35).

The Expected Suffering

The disciples struggled with what must have seemed to be a puzzling contradiction in Jesus' teaching. Yet it is clear from what preceded that it was no mystery to God. Jesus suffered and denied himself; so must his followers. It is responsible self-denial which gladly substitutes divine interests for self-interests even when its objects are sinners: "love one another" (John 15:12).

In John 10 we read that Christ knows his own, calls them *by name* and leads them forth. Only his own know his voice.

Only his own follow him. Not only are these friends chosen but that choosing constitutes an appointment, a commissioning. That is, it places obligations upon those who are chosen. We cannot be Christians without being obligated to God. In John 15:12-14 it may sound as if Jesus is talking about voluntary obedience. But it is clear that he is talking about obligatory obedience. Further, that commissioning is that we should be active--that is, "go." A car cannot move in neutral. A Christian is called, appointed, obligated to be in gear, to progress.

The goal of this activity is enduring fruit. We take this to mean growth in grace. In the immediate context Jesus appears to be talking about fruits from the Spirit: especially, as expressed in a proper relationship to God, (v. 14), fellow Christians (vv. 12, 13), and the world of unbelievers (vv. 18-27). Also, we cannot help but include here the cultivation of the fruit of the Spirit: love, joy, peace, longsuffering, goodness, kindness, faithfulness, gentleness, self-control (Gal. 5:22, 23). Being thus gifted with fruit of the Spirit we are obligated to cultivate that fruit as we use our time, talent, personality, and finances in promoting Christ's church (cf., I Cor. 12).

After we have denied ourselves and have been commissioned to bear fruit we then have become friends of God. However, we must then always remember that the friends of God are no friends of the present world order and those who are committed to it. Since, as God's friends, we are appointed to new attitudes and actions—a new life-style—the world will not understand us. Even as the world hated Jesus, so also will the world hate his friends. They hated him first (John 15:18). The basis of their hatred is our new nature which results from divine election (v. 19). As water douses fire, and light banishes darkness, so the ungodly by their hostile nature oppose the godly to do away with them. This should be no surprise to us, however, since a slave is no greater than his master (v. 20). If we obey our commission (Matt. 28:18-20) we, too, will be hated without cause. Surely, it is clear that to be a friend of God is to be an enemy of the world both in our attitude toward its lifestyle and in their reaction to our persons. Note well that they hate *us* and we hate their lifestyle (that is, sin).

Lastly the friends of God are witnesses of Christ and the lifestyle he commands (John 15:26-27). Jesus tells his disciples that this opposition to the world will not stop when he departs. The Holy Spirit whom he will send to dwell in them (John 14:26) will bear witness of him. His disciples, being thus indwelt, will also bear witness of Jesus. In the Book of Acts the Holy Spirit extends this task of witnessing about Christ to the entire church (Acts 1:8; 8:1, 4).

Thus, although the disciples were slow to understand, Jesus taught them (and us) that following him necessarily involves a new lifestyle. This lifestyle demands self-sacrifice in every realm of living. One much emphasized result is the hatred the world will show to the Christian lifestyle. They will hate us without cause. Indeed, even fellow Christians who conceive life according to ungodly patterns (i.e., who are rebellious against God's law or its implications) will hate us.

2. Witness and Child-raising

How do the above principles effect our responsibility to our children? Part of our responsibility to obey God's commandment of love is to communicate our commitment by our attitudes, actions, and teaching. The responsibility to be faithful in these things finds special focus in our task of child-raising. There are many biblical passages that show this clearly, but we will consider the foundational passage: Deuteronomy 6. This passage states, as a command, for the Old Testament church, what God requires of parents who will bring up their children God's way. "You shall teach them [God's words] diligently to your children. This covenantal responsibility which Abraham followed by faith and which Moses commanded of the Israelites must also be *our* responsibility *today*. "Fathers, do not exasperate your children;

87

instead, bring them up in the training and instruction of the Lord" (Eph. 6:4)[1] We must realize that a very important part of our love for God in the new age is shown when we fulfill our responsibility to train our children in godliness. This should be part of our new lifestyle.

The final verses of Deuteronomy 6 (20-25) show how the instruction in total submission to one Lord with all our heart is strongly focused on the children of the covenant (i.e., children whose parents are Christians and have received God's promises, and have been given the responsibility of teaching them to their children--Acts 2:38-39). The biblical emphasis is that child-raising and training are a very important part of our obligation to God. In verse 20 we see that the attitudes and actions of parents who obey God's covenant elicit questions from covenant children.

The answer given to children is summarized in verses 21-25. First, they are to be told that all the covenant participants (believers belonging to the Christian community with their children) have is a gift from God. As God's grace called Israel out of slavery in Egypt, similarly, his grace called all believers from their slavery to sin. Egypt's slavery was not simply spiritual; it bound them in every aspect of their family life and their occupation. So too, our slavery to sin bound us in every aspect of life. God's power effected the delivery. There is no mistaking this emphasis on God's absolute control of nature, men and nations in delivering his people (v. 22). Is God any less active today? Certainly, he is not! How can we explain our present situation apart from the marvelous activity of God in, with, through, and for his church? God's providence effected the present blessings. Israel's children throughout the history of the nation were to learn that the land, the produce of the land, and the society in which they lived, were blessings from God and were to be responsibly governed and ordered by God's Word. Children

1 . Other significant passages: Col. 3:20-21; II Cor. 12:14; I Thess. 1:11; I Tim. 3:4, 12; Titus 1:6; Mark 10:13-16.

are also to be clearly instructed that all God has done to his people and required of them is for their own good. Verse 24 summarizes this by noting that children are to be told that observance of *all* his commandments works for their own good and survival. In other words, the first reason for obedience is their earthly well-being and the second, their eternal well-being. The two cannot be separated. Indeed, the earthly well-being of every man is related directly to his obedience to God's Word. We as Christians are the salt and light of the world. It is only as we are obediently repenting and believing through Jesus Christ that we are truly the salt of the earth. Further, it is only as we know and keep God's commandments as a preparation for eternal life that we express our eternal life here and pierce the darkness around us with God's light. It is as part of this fulfillment of the God-given mission of Christians that Christian schools are needed. Deuteronomy 6 says that all this is the responsibility of parents as they rear their children. The responsibility includes communicating the content of our Christian faith and heritage, but over and above this, we must also communicate to the world an entirely God-centered view of life.

3. Conclusion

The study presented above is intended to indicate why it is necessary for believers to think in terms of self-sacrifice when contemplating responsible child-raising. The disciples did not expect self-denial and suffering to be a continuing feature of kingdom living, but Christ Jesus taught that it was. He said his friends (disciples) are only those who obey him, who have been chosen and appointed to that obedience, and whose obedience takes the form of a lifestyle foreign to and hated by those in rebellion against God. Their entire lifestyle and confession will witness of him, for new life effected by spiritual regeneration necessarily involves self-sacrifice in every realm of living. The more obedient we are to our Lord, the more sacrifice seems to be involved.

89

Then we concentrated on one aspect of obedience to God's covenant; namely, child-raising. Love for God obligates one's family to obedience to God's covenant. Thus, biblical "love" is inseparable from God's law which is to be carefully taught to one's children. Love governs our attitudes and actions and necessitates carefully planned education of our children. The self-sacrifice so integrally bound to Christian living is no less a governing principle in child-raising.

What Are the Things Which We Should Be Willing To Sacrifice for the Christian Education of Our Children?

We now want to look at how the various participants in the Christian day school uniquely demonstrate their willingness to deny self and serve Christ.

1. The Teacher

How does the teacher in a Christian school bear witness? Here we want to examine the teacher's self-denial as exhibited in his or her sacrifice in finances, prestige, training, public life, and ministry.

Financial Sacrifice

The teacher in a Christian day school usually does not get wages comparable to those paid public school teachers. Often the difference is considerable. This difference is translated, of course, into the lack of spending power. The teacher willingly accepts this difference in a day when the public school teachers are pressing for more and more wages even in the face of court injunctions and rapid inflation. This makes a striking witness of the teacher's dedication to Christian education. If the teacher is supporting a household, this lower wage can mean a lot of "doing without." The teacher willingly faces stringent living conditions and sometimes a near-poverty level living standard. The teacher does this even though he is highly educated and lives in a society where such voluntary rejection of materialism is considered to be quite undesirable. Furthermore, teachers in Christian schools often put in longer hours, work with much poorer equipment (sometimes with no equipment at all), and are, among other things, expected to do a better job than their higher paid counterparts in the public school. Even unmarried teachers are willing to accept the job at a much lower pay level than their counterparts in the public school. Both married and unmarried teachers should reject materialism and give of their talents as a clear public witness of their love for their Lord.

Sacrifice in Prestige

A teacher in a Christian school should exhibit self-denial and obedience to Christ by enduring a loss of prestige. Previously we discussed "institutional" prejudice. Those hateful attitudes which the world has toward Christ and his followers are often felt about the teacher in the Christian school. Social prestige is usually one of the chief rewards of being a school teacher. A teacher in a Christian school, if he does not know it from the beginning, soon learns that he receives little respect from the world. As a matter of fact, the teacher in a Christian school often is looked down upon as having taken a job in the Christian school because he was unqualified to do anything else.

Sacrifice in Training

Another area where teachers in Christian schools exhibit self-sacrifice is in the area of their training. First, they need a double education because they are responsible for knowing the "secular" position as well as the Christian position. Secondly, they need a "deeper" education than the teacher in a public school. A teacher in a Christian school, being responsible to present both the religious and cultural aspects of covenantal obedience, must constantly examine the assumptions underlying all textbooks, films, and other instructional materials which are to be used. Teachers will find themselves struggling against their own unbiblical assumptions. Often the textbooks available are built on anti-biblical assumptions and attractively and cleverly present unbelief. The teacher in a Christian school must discern such things. When teaching, it is also necessary for the teacher to perceive the assumptions upon which the students build their concepts. Thus, in preparing and delivering their materials our teachers need more philosophical maturity than a "secular" teacher needs. Of course, no religious depth is required in the public school at all, whereas in the Christian school the teacher must meet a great variety of "Christian" approaches both from the children and parents and is called to guide both into a more consistent and mature walk with the Lord. The conscientious teacher in a Christian school also faces a good deal of re-education. He not only needs to learn *how* to teach, but *what* to teach. This task is especially difficult since often there is little or no help in the textbooks.

Sacrifice as a Public Person

The teacher in a Christian school is called to face closer and more public scrutiny than the public school teacher. Whether married or single, he represents Christ in a special way. If he does not recognize this and accept it from the beginning, the results can seriously mar the testimony and effectiveness of the school. If it is accepted and joyfully engaged, then their Christian commitment is greatly enhanced. In some areas of the country this "public examination" may not appear to be as important as in others. It is especially evident where the school is a new or small enterprise.

The teacher also faces closer scrutiny by the administration and Christian community. If biblical standards are being pursued, both the administration and the supporting families will be concerned that the teacher is doing his best. Both in and out of the classroom the teacher is expected to pursue with maturity both the "religious" and "cultural" aspects of the covenant. (How many public school teachers are expected to practice the highest ideals of biblical morality and are counseled if they fail to do so? How many of them are expected to be a spiritual example in the local church? None of them, of course!) Now perhaps this is not the situation in every Christian school, but it is in many of them. It should be our hope for the future that all of our Christian school teachers may be faultless in their public witness before all men.

Sacrifice in Ministry

This is really the summary of all that precedes and all that could be added. What we have said is that a teacher in a Christian school is called upon to enter a ministry. This is a ministry in the "classical" sense of the term, that is, someone doing something for God because he believes in the task and is doing it even at the cost of great personal denial. The Bible calls every Christian to conceive of his life as such a ministry (Mark 8:34). Most of us, however, get taken up with pursuits of pleasure, self-satisfaction, and personal isolationism. For a long time the only "minister" in many local churches has been the teaching elder, the pastor. He has been expected to live on less income, and give of himself and his family without reservation and without complaint. He is expected to be ready anywhere and anytime to render help. He is expected to be a leader and an example in good times and bad. This same structure now extends to a teacher in a Christian school. He is a "minister." His area of responsibility differs from that of the teaching elder. He does a different job, but the dedication and self-denial required are similar. It would be good if the entire church were to begin to live the same way. How much more time, talent, and money would be available for the work of the Lord in the church and the school if this were the case? What a joyous thing it would be, indeed, if every church member would apply the same standards in his own life.

Certainly the teacher's willing and joyful example in all these areas is a testimony to all who see his willing self-denial and obedience to Christ in everything.

2. The Parent

The Christian parents who send their children to the Christian school and who form the basic supporting community of the school willingly endure much self-denial which publicly declares their love for the Lord.

One area where this self-denial is manifested is the financial area. Paying tuition often means considerable sacrifice. In our local situation it means eating less meat, buying fewer clothes, foregoing vacations, working overtime, and using old equipment. Everyday spending must be curtailed to meet the tuition payments. In a society motivated by luxury and fulfilling one's wants, the practice of Christian families stands out boldly. The result of this self-denial is closer family cooperation and greater happiness in seeing goals which have been worked for, accomplished. The financial sacrifice reaps untold benefits. Of course, one of the greatest of these is hearing one's seven-year-old son explain with real insight the story of the ark, the purpose of discipline, and the meaning of "love your neighbor," as well as experiencing the joy of seeing him grow in his understanding of God's covenant and its requirements because of what he is learning in school. It is worth every effort to know that the school is leading him toward salvation and service rather than away from it. The world and other Christians see this witness, too. They know how hard it would be for them to pay tuition in addition to tithes, offerings, and taxes. They also know that they would not be willing to do this unless they really believed strongly in the school.

The parents also attest their willingness to obey the Lord

94

by giving of their time. The Christian school enterprise requires parents to be more active in running the school, fund raising, and sometimes, janitorial service. Most Americans have come to the place where they let others run the schools. Perhaps they attend PTA meetings but few get involved beyond that. The parent interested in a Christian school, however, finds such detachment nearly impossible and highly impractical. If the school is to survive, it requires everyone's help.

The parents who support a Christian school must be very involved in running the school. Board members are parents who learn to do the job. Perhaps some have special talents like bookkeeping or a training in education, but many of them must learn their job as they go. Moreover, their task in general involves getting into deep philosophical and theological issues. This requires much deep thinking and studying. Thus their task may involve consulting with people who are experienced in education, Christian schools, plant operation and needs, curriculum development, hiring teachers, drafting constitutions and bookkeeping. It is a lot of work, but the product is a great growth in faith and a more effective witness for the Lord. In the association, the parents who are the basic support of the school are called upon to face many crucial decisions, but through all this there is a lot of opportunity to witness openly to friends of the school and to parents who have a limited view of Christianity.

Fund raising also involves almost every parent. This is a matter of necessity. Regardless of the cost of tuition it is seldom adequate to meet all the expenses of the school. In most cases there are few "angels" who can pay the difference. So parents and other interested supporters must engage in fund raising projects. These projects require a great deal of time. The result is the continuation of the school and a greatly extended witness for the Lord.

These fund raising projects allow mature Christians to work for a common goal along with the immature Christians and the non-Christians who send their children to the school. We have an opportunity to live our commitment before them. They see us react under stress. They hear us talk about the Lord's business. They see the husband and wife work together probably in a way they wished was typical of their own family. They hear theological and ethical discussions, often from a perspective that they have never before heard. Perhaps these discussions will lead them to consider that which they had never really considered. They hear our prayers. Our witness extends to everything we are and do. As we work together we exhibit to the objects of our witness almost every detail of Christian commitment. And, significantly, this occurs in a context of great self-denial and joyful cooperation.

It is not only to those with whom we work and those within the supporting church community that we bear witness, however. It is also before the eyes of the entire community. These are the people who will know our self-sacrifice and dedication. In our community, for example, the dedication, love and self-sacrifice of the Christian school community has extended for miles throughout the countryside. The witness is very positive, expecially since many parents involved are not from the orthodox evangelical community. They may not understand, and may even dislike, our doctrine but they cannot deny our love for them and our love for their children. Gossip in small towns is legendary and in the past has mercilessly defamed the Christian community, but now the grapevine will be able to carry strongly contradictory reports. Those who have never worked with us continue their defaming, but those who are involved in the school (and often their friends and relatives) are beginning to defend our school and our love for them. All this and much more is a result of our working together in seeking to raise funds for the school. What a witness it has been to the world!

Parents attest their obedience and self-denial in the area of prestige. As a school grows and shows that it is a going concern, its reputation as a good teaching center may become well established. At the beginning, however, the school appears to be a rather makeshift enterprise. It usually meets in a church basement where the facilities are far from ideal. The teachers are probably young and inexperienced. The board of education appears quite ill-equipped for their task. The parents know that appearances are deceptive; they know the dedication of all involved, and even more, they know that their Christian perspective on life and education will make a superior school.

The self-denial and obedience of parents is also attested when they are asked why they have their children in the school. The response will probably focus on the benefits seen in the lives of the children, and in this way the questioner "hears" what the parents are doing. Also, their obedience contrasts considerably with the incessant complaints which other parents level against the public school system. At great financial sacrifice Christian parents have put their children in a school where the academic standards are absolutes (children are given "real" grades rather than pats on their academic heads), where all the teachers are responsible to do a good job in the classroom and live an upright life outside the classroom, where rebellion and insolence are met with firm and loving discipline, and where the child is taught Christian morality and religion.

Thus, parents amply attest true Christian denial of sin and affirm their obedience to Christ.

3. The Church

There are many ways by which a church can bear strong witness to the world by having a Christian school on its premises. First, financially the school often requires direct or indirect support from the church. Indirectly, the same constituency forms the financial base of both institutions. This may cut into the money available for church projects (home and foreign missions, etc.), although the reverse has also been true in many cases. Direct support of the school may take many forms. Ideally, the church will put the school in its budget. Incidental support from the church can include hidden costs such as heating, electricity, and wear and tear on the building. The church also may experience a draining-off of the talent and energies of its best leadership. However, in our local situation the school has developed much more leadership than it has drained off. By willingly housing and promoting the school, the church publicly declares its concern for children in a day when the public school and family life are rapidly deteriorating. Another important thrust of this public witness of the church is its clear declaration of its concern to promote and defend the truth.

4. The Pupil

One of the most effective declarations of the value of a Christian school is the effect the school has on the life and development of the students. They are closely watched by friends and relatives. In our local area almost every student has shown marked and extremely good progress in social adjustment and academic achievement. This is what one expects a Christian school to do, and when it actually happens it is most exciting. All levels of students exhibit the same laudable qualities, from those who were having trouble in the public school and were sent to the Christian school for special help, to the average or above average student sent by parents who believe in *Christian* education. The teachers spend more time with each student, show more concern for each one, and generally seem to get good responses from them. The product of a Christian school is a more mature child whose understanding of Christianity is superior to that of children educated in the public school. They are also better disciplined, more mannerly, and better socially adjusted than many (if not most) of their contemporaries. There may be particular exceptions to the above description, but our experience so far has been surprisingly uniform. Later, as the child matures, he will come to realize that he has had a more "honest" education. He has been presented with both "sides." Hopefully, it will be possible to keep the child in a Christian school throughout his entire education, but even if this is not possible the benefits of training him in an atmosphere of the truth (even for a limited period) cannot be denied. The unbelieving child may rebel, but the child who becomes a believer will come to thank his parents and his church for their self-denial and covenantal obedience. Later, he will look back joyfully on whatever self-denial he may have experienced (being separated from most of the kids in his neighborhood, not having a gymnasium or band in the school he attends, etc.) and be grateful for his awareness of the nature and extent of sin, the world, and Christian responsibility.

E. Conclusion

One purpose for having a Christian school is to show the world the willingness of teacher, parent, church, and student to deny sin and self and follow Christ in everything. This must be exhibited and pursued in every facet of the school. In this section we saw, in ways the world clearly understands, how each participant in the school fulfills this purpose. The Christian school is truly a strong instrument in communicating our commitment to our Lord and our denial of sin.

What Will These Sacrifices Say About Us to the People Who Watch?

The principles which previously have been set forth in this chapter and in the preceding chapters of this volume point strongly to the desirability of Christian schools consciously structured on a consistently biblical basis. Let us now consider more closely the object of our witness. The proposition which we are discussing stipulates the "world" as that object. What follows is a discussion of the biblical concept "world" as it relates specifically to Christian witness. Our witness does not aim, however, nor should it be aimed only at non-Christians. We should witness to "worldly" Christians, one another, and our own children that we are unreservedly willing to deny sin and be obedient to Christ.

1. The World

Our witness in establishing and maintaining Christian schools is a public declaration of our servanthood to Christ. The principle of servanthood is given to us by God, and as Christian parents this is expressed when we take up our responsibility to make sure that our children are taught the *truth*. This is part of our witnessing of Christ (John 15:27; Acts 1:8) to the "world." The "world" consists of unbelievers, all of whom are blind to the *truth* in Christ, hate the truth (Christ), and serve their father the Devil. Even though the kingdom of Satan is strong, Christ is stronger and has overcome it (John 16:33). Therefore, believers need not fear. We can and should proceed to witness and push back the Devil's attacks upon the truth.

The "world" is not neutral toward the things of God. The degree and vigor of conscious opposition may well be proportional to the degree to which the "truth" is forced upon them, but the rebellion against the truth is never absent (Rom. 1:18ff.). Christ taught that the "world" would especially hate the truth and those who practice and propogate it:

> If the world hateth you, ye know that it hath
> hated me before it hated you. If ye were of the
> world, the world would love its own: but because
> ye are not of the world, but I chose you out of
> the world, therefore the world hateth you
>
> (John 15:18-19).

God is truth (Deut. 32:4); Jesus is the truth (John 8:46; 14:6); and the Holy Spirit is the Spirit of truth (John 16:13).

What God says is true and men ought to receive it. As the truth is proclaimed the world reacts with hostility and the world's true nature clearly surfaces.

How does the world express its hatred of the "truth"? One way is that they seem to ignore the truth. We say "seem to" because they cannot truly ignore it.

First, the general law of God in the realm of ethics and morality is clearly written on their hearts and their consciences and attests the fact that they both know and agree with it (Rom. 2:14, 15). This is not to say that they know in detail the specifics of the law. God has chosen not to reveal them to the world. However, what they do know they willfully reject and replace with laws which please themselves. Furthermore, when they do set up specific laws of morality and condemn others for not conforming to those laws they attest that they feel God's law is binding upon man, including themselves (Rom. 2:1). Not every specific law they set up conforms to what God has decreed is lawful, but the general lines of their law do conform to it. Hence, that which does not conform to God's truth is a conscious willful deviation from the truth, rebellion against God ("they exchanged the truth of God for a lie." Rom. 1:25). *Now if the world in its structuring of schools "ignores" what they know and believe to be true, they are not simply "ignoring," they are "rebelling."*

Secondly, the creation shouts forth and clearly declares the glory and nature of God (Rom. 1:18ff.; Ps. 19). This speaks of "cultural education." *When the public school does not accept the biblical view of history, literature, and biology, the public school is not simply ignoring God; it is openly rebelling against what is clearly manifested.* The biblical view of education should cause the students to become aware of how each subject they study exhibits the glory of God. However, in contrast to this, the public school teaches the students a lie, indeed a constant torrent of lies. They are teaching contrary to the truth.

101

Finally, both of these factors attest to true religion. All men know not just any concept of God, but the God who reveals himself in their heart, creation, and the Scriptures. They do not, however, glorify or thank him, but they create a religion that suits their own taste (Rom. 1:21-23). The God of the Bible is the Lord of all and proclaims himself to be such. *When the public schools do not promote true religion they promote false religion.* Theirs is a religion that makes man the creator, the saviour, the judge of life, the determiner of right and wrong, the lord of history, and the object of worship.

Today, the leaders of our country and the public schools are once again proclaiming that salvation comes from man. Man is presented as the final judge over human life. No longer are our children being forced to deal with moral issues which are shaded in grays, but now, even worse, they are urged to make wrong conclusions about moral issues which are clearly defined in black and white. Children in our public schools are taught that men and women have a right to do whatever they want with their own bodies. (The body, however, belongs to God—I Cor. 6:19.) Since a fetus is part of one's body, one can do with "it" whatever he desires. Therefore, abortion is a matter of private conscience and not of divine, or even public, law. How can a child who has been taught from kindergarten to high school that religion has no right to speak and nothing to say, come to a biblical decision on abortion? To do so he must surmount his own beliefs, inculcated largely by our public education system, that his body is his own. Even many mature Christians feel that what their child does is ultimately a matter for him to decide and that he ought not to be forced into the right way. Moreover, the child must also surmount the disapproval of his peers. Finally, the child must go against his *teacher* and do so without going against all that is taught. If the child is faced with a school system which teaches the principles we have stated above, it would take an extremely spiritually alert child to come to a biblical decision with regard to the abortion issue. As parents we cannot expect our children to be able to withstand such terrible pressure, and there can be no doubt that we must all fight against a public education system which spreads such godless principles.

Thus, man is presented as the judge and determiner of morality when biblical principles are swept aside and the child is taught that he has the right to decide in all areas what he can and should do with his life and with his body. This is only one among many ways in which unbiblical morality is taught in the classroom.

Man is also presented as the lord of history when history is represented as the record of man's (not God's) walk through time, and it is clearly pointed out that *man* is advancing. It is alleged that things are getting better and better, due to the advances in science and technology.

Finally, although there are many more false religious doctrines taught in the public schools, man is presented as the sole object of worship. Our children have a natural inclination toward this as is evidenced by their adoration of sports and movie heroes. The public school leads the child even more subtly to conclude that the only hope for the world is mankind and his ability to reason. All that relates to God is depicted as unknown, uncertain, or wrong, while *man* offers the only real hope and help. This describes what we might call "humanism." Many who are advocates of this "religion" do not admit being consciously hostile to Christianity. Often they are unaware of the nature of the truth in the sense that they cannot articulate the doctrines presented in the Scriptures.

In some areas of social organization the church or any Christian organization is dismissed or derided as a viable option. For example, the public schools often leave the child with the idea that the church is a carry-over from the days when men did not know any better. It is built on ignorance and opposed to all human advancement. When a child states

103

his belief in God and the Bible he is openly rebuked, often by being politely "put down" by the teacher's attitude.

Moreover, hostility toward Christian schools is often expressed because they are viewed as inferior. Sometimes this judgment is just—especially, in the case of neo-fundamentalist schools, many of which openly state that they are not really interested in academics. For example, this writer knows of parents who were told by administrators of a Christian school that their school does not meet good academic standards and that this should not really bother Christians since the "religious" aspect is the most important anyway. In another case, the authorities censor every thought and concept that is presented to the students; the children never see the world as it truly is. We are not advocating showing the child all the vileness of the world, but he should be shown what the world is doing and why it is wrong, for example, in such areas as evolution and abortion. Although the world's condemnation of Christian schools is warranted in some instances, it is not just in most instances.

There are many Christian schools built upon the truth which do a superior job in training children. If this is so, why do even Christians within orthodox churches so often feel that church related schools cannot do the job of education adequately? The first reason is the seeming failure of Christian schools to do the job parents expect them to do. We must note here that schools built on orthodox principles do not necessarily communicate these principles to the child. Parents sometimes expect the school to do their job, or even the job of the Holy Spirit. If children do not get the message, these parents may conclude that the school should be closed. That is like killing the doctor who specializes in cancer because most of his patients die of cancer. However, the negative results of a Christian education in the life of a particular child do not negate the principal obligation of having a Christian school. *The problem is not with the idea of having a school; it is with the way a particular school is operated.* In this case the proper procedure is to look more carefully at

104

whether or not biblical principles are being carried out in the classroom.

The second reason some Christians conclude that there should be no Christian day schools is that they may be a product of institutional prejudice. They have come to their conclusion because they accept the institutional hostility of the world. In some areas of the country this institutional hostility is translated into laws which are prejudicial against the establishment and maintenance of Christian schools.

Open hostility may develop into persecuting hostility. This is what occured in the case of our Lord. He talked of the hatred from the world (John 15) and on the very same night he was arrested (John 18). The history of the church is sprinkled with periods of persecution. Already today there are minor expressions of persecutions in cases where, for example, the state regulations for Christian school buildings are beyond the material means of those supporting them. Let us pray that this not a harbinger of more pronounced and extensive persecution.

2. The Worldly

The witness we set forth by establishing Christian schools is not only to the world (non-Christians) but it is also to the "worldly." By this we mean Christians with limited views of Christianity. That such Christians exist is evident from the Bible. Jesus set forth the guidelines in defining "worldliness" when in the parable of the sower he declares that some who had heard the word received it and made professions of faith, but that the cares of the world and the deceitfulness of the flesh grew up choking out the plant of faith (Matt. 13:22). To turn back to the thoughts and life patterns which typify unbelief is to be friendly to the world and to be hostile to God (James 1:14). Such friendship consists of being guided by the lusts of the flesh, the desires of the mind (Eph. 2:3). There are several lists of the works of the flesh (I John 2:15, 16; Ga. 5:19-21). While most Christians are quite aware of such evils, many Christians are unaware of the full extent of the "religious" and "cultural" aspects of these evils. Therefore, they do not recognize that "worldliness" is a way of thinking and acting that restricts the Lordship of God by narrowly limiting it to ethical, personal religion, and church related activities. *The Christian school tells such Christians that there is much more to God's demands than they think.* It summons them to deeper reflection and renewed dedication.

Believers are urged to hold firm to the truth and not to love the world (I John 2:15-17). "Worldliness" is a most undesirable quality. Peter wrote that those who become entangled again in the world enter a state worse than that in which they lived before their profession of faith (II Peter 2:20ff.). This is nothing to toy with. If we love our fellow Christians as we ought (John 15:17), we certainly want them to avoid worldliness. One good way to summon them to total commitment and thoroughgoing obedience is by establishing Christian day schools and then challenging them to join us in more perfect obedience.

In summary then, we can testify to "worldly" Christians as to the more correct concepts of denial of sin and obedience to Christ by operating a Christian school. But let us give a note of caution here. Many Christians have "bought" the view of worldliness which narrowly identifies it with using tobacco, drinking alcoholic beverages and going to the movie theatres. This really misses the point of the biblical doctrine of worldliness. First of all, this adds to God's law by making man's conclusions God's Word. Some of the "don'ts" may be wise, but we dare not add to the law by making what may be wise and expedient binding on other men's consciences. Secondly, this view, like that of the Pharisees, does much of what should be done but does it often at the expense of the "weightier" matters (Matt. 23:23). Still other Christians, although not caught up in this particular error, have limited "cultural" obedience by making much of what they do "neutral." They are truly taken up with the cares of this present world. It is to such people that we witness in the Christian school. In the Christian school we have an opportunity to show, and often tell, of the richness, the breadth, and the depth of the truth. To both groups we attest our zeal and commitment to carry out a total life of confrontation with the present evil world.

3. The Christians

By establishing and maintaining Christian schools we bear witness to those Christians who are zealous for full life obedience to God. It would be wrong to assume that we do not need one another's example of obedience. We are not always as consistent and strong as we should be. Like the members of "Weight Watchers" we may know our problem and the solution, but need the help and example of others like ourselves to do what we need to do. Even more importantly, the school provides a forum where we can pursue the implications of obedience. At least in one local situation, many Christians first became aware of the idea of life service for God through the decision-making process which resulted in the establishment of a Christian school.

Furthermore, since the sermons and other teaching in the church program focus specifically on religious education, there is little opportunity to engage in cultural education. Through the Christian day school, however, trained leaders will have a forum to educate the Christian public in the breadth and depth of obedience to our Lord. Thus, the school is a means whereby we can upbuild and therefore strengthen one another by mutual example and exhortation.

We have had a school for five years and each year the strength and numbers of the congregation of the local church have increased. Families have been shown just how deeply others are committed and they have been encouraged and summoned to more consistent living for the Lord. The church has reaped untold and probably yet unknown benefits. There are many areas where the beneficial effect of the school on the Christian community is clearly seen. One such area is the attendance in Sunday school and worship services. The Sunday school has increased by 30 percent, morning worship by 50 percent and evening worship by 100 percent. Now, not all of that represents Christians who have become more aware of their greater need for formal instruction, but much of it does. Another such area is in the church's income; it has more than doubled since the school began and this is in addition to the school budget. In our context, it would be hard to argue that the school has not *effectively* witnessed to Christians about their covenantal responsibilities and guided them to obedience.

4. The Children of the Covenant

One very significant witness is that which we give to our own children. Having them in a Christian school will not guarantee that they will become Christians. It will, however, guarantee that they will get a clearer picture of our concern for them, or our responsibility before God, and our willingness to carry out that responsibility.

Our children see our concern for them when we send them to a Christian school. Often sending them involves considerable self-sacrifice. If we accept our role as being responsible for our child's development and learning, this will always propel us into active involvement in the school structure. We will attend the meetings and voice our opinion. We will confer with the teacher and seek to help him both by constructive criticism and active cooperation. The school and our children will often be in our family and public prayers. Thus, the child will see the concern of his own parents and of the whole church. Such a concrete expression of deep and self-sacrificing concern attests our deep love for him and constitutes a strong witness to him.

Our children more clearly see our responsibility before God by spending the most alert hours of their day under Christian teaching, where the truth is probably communicated as much by example as by precept.

One cannot help asking what kind of an example is shown to children in the public schools. What do the relationships between men and women show the child? Are women in submission to men without being non-persons? What is the relationship to God that is communicated? Is the responsibility of being a servant of God consistently depicted before the child? Is God consciously recognized as the Lord of every thought and action? Is life presented as a working out of covenantal obedience? Are the truths of the Bible viewed as binding and taught as imperatives? To ask such questions is to give the answers. In the Christian school we have the privilege of expressing the fullness of our responsibility before the child on a level which he can grasp. Can there be any question as to the desirability and advisability of such a witness?

Our children see our willingness to obey our Lord when we send them to a Christian school. Of course, even if we do not have children or are unable to send our own children, we show the covenant youth that we recognize our responsibility when we support the Christian school. Can there really be any doubt about the all-pervading commands of our Lord? Certainly there cannot be. We clearly declare this when we support the Christian school. What a witness it is to the child to see grandparents and members of the church sacrificially giving and working for the school. When we do such tasks willingly and joyfully we not only show our concern for the child but we show him just how much we are willing to do for the Lord. We show the child Christianity in action. Moreover, the teachers, as our representatives live before the child and display a mature Christian life while at the same time they are concerned with the ABC's as well as other weightier matters. These teachers are so concerned about this ministry of education that they are willing to sacrifice greatly.

Through all these things which happen in the Christian school the child sees a concrete, living expression of Christian dedication to God's commands.

5. Conclusion

To whom is our witness? If we carry out proper Christian education, our witness is, indeed, to the whole world. That is what we should want and pray for. We witness to the "world"—those who are unbelievers and may not see that Christianity is a way of living and thinking. The world ultimately knows the truth and may even hostiley react to it when faced with it. Our desire is not to create hostility, however; it is to make the truth clearer to them. We witness to the "worldly"—Christians whose view of truth is distorted and confined. This is especially true here in America where the public schools are getting more money and doing an increasingly inadequate job while on the other hand the Christian school with much less money turns out a much better product and thus speaks to "worldly" Christians in a way that they can understand quite clearly. We witness to one another and, finally but not least, we witness to our children through the school. In view of these many benefits and many more which could be mentioned, it ought to be agreed that the Christian day school is most desirable indeed, and worthy of much self-sacrifice.

How High a Priority Should Christian Education Have?

If the Christian school is a clear implication, if not a demand, of covenantal obedience, and if it is an effective witness, then to what degree should we pursue establishing and maintaining such a school? It is our contention that the Christian community should exert great effort to establish and maintain a school. Yet we should not conclude that a Christian school must have supreme priority.

110

Having a Christian school is a strong implication of the covenant, but not a command of it. The difference between "strong implication" and "command" is one of necessity: namely, is one breaking God's Word if his child is not in a Christian school which teaches the biblical position? In other words, should the church discipline parents whose children are not in such a school? Again, should a congregation be disciplined if its children are not provided with such a school? We think not. Our reasons for this conclusion are: first, there is no clear biblical command which specifically enunciates that the *only* way to fulfill our obligation to train our children is to establish a Christian school. Second, there are alternative ways to educate our children in the requirements and content of covenantal revelation, for example, special after school or Saturday classes (as practiced by many Jewish communities), or special concern and effort by parents to augment the child's instruction in the home with pointedly Christian viewpoints in specific areas and issues.

While having a properly-based school is not a luxury that can be cavalierly set aside, neither is it a necessity which demands absolute obedience. It is a highly desirable enterprise which allows us to carry out our responsibility and witness very effectively. We might say that having a school based on biblical principles is a "need" of the Christian family and community.

This "need" is pressing enough in our society to warrant great self-sacrifice. We can never lose sight of it in planning our lives. This is especially true with reference to where we locate our families. We should think very carefully before moving into an area where there is no Christian school. But, if we do live in an area where there is no Christian school, we have several alternatives. Let us emphasize that as parents it is our responsibility to see that our children are trained in covenantal content and obedience. This puts a lot of work on our shoulders. In areas without a Christian school, we will need to consult with our pastor quite carefully. It may be that we might interest him in conducting special instruction classes for our children and ourselves. These classes should seek to detail the specific application of the religious and cultural aspects of the covenant to our own lives and to our children's lives. Parents should be eager to study the Bible and other books which will help them in this task. This might mean operating a book table, bookstore, or book-of-the-month club with at least one evening a month set aside to discuss a book. Even this is hardly enough, but it is a start. If we really take our responsibility seriously, we will seek to get much more help from our pastor. Perhaps we should try to establish a family conference (including all interested families) once a week. These conferences could involve the parents and the pastor reading the textbooks their children use in the school and then seeking together to point out the problems therein, and later to try to instruct the children in a correct biblical interpretation. To the best of our knowledge this approach to Christian education has not yet been pursued in the Christian community. In areas where there is no Christian school, parents cannot responsibly relinquish the education of their children to others; they have a great responsibility and much work to do.

If we have no school, we cannot sacrifice the command of the Great Commission in order to have enough resources to start a school (Matt. 28:18-20). The Bible sets forth the spreading of the gospel as a very urgent matter and therefore we must not lower its prime importance in the work of our Christian community. It is true that part of the discipling of the nations is "teaching them to do *all*" Christ's commands, which is a major goal of the Christian school. Yet if we must choose between pastor or school teacher, church building or school building, and between foreign missions budget or Christian school, those projects directly related to the work of the church must come first.

However, we must not emphasize the work of the organized church in such a way as to ignore Christian schools. This is a real danger in some circles. We see this in the endeavors of many Christian communities where there is great enthusiasm about missions but there appears to be relatively little interest in the cultural mandate to subdue, cultivate, and rule in the earth (Gen. 1:27, 28; 2:15). It is the duty of every Christian to pursue both areas of responsibility. The Great Commission is in a sense primary, but the cultural mandate is *no less binding*. It is probably more work to pursue the cultural mandate (at least in a sense) because most of us are thoroughly indoctrinated in a secular culture. This in no way lightens our responsibility. With reference to Christian schools, our indoctrination, if recognized, should lead us to yearn to see our covenant children trained in the things of God.

This question of how far our commitment to Christian education should go arises when we think that it is possible for the state to become hostile to the truth. At present the state teaches unbelief as the official state position, but it tolerates belief by not pointedly and actively attacking it. What should Christians do if the state begins condemning our Christian beliefs (as under Communism or Nazism)? We will have to face the problem when it arises, but it will not be an easy decision. What should we do if the state by law requires high standards in educational equipment, plant facilities and teacher salaries? In effect, this sort of regulation would force the private Christian school out of existence. Each Christian community will have to determine its own needs, necessities and luxuries. It might be that many things we call "needs" are really "luxuries" and we will just have to place the "need" for a properly based school before these "luxuries." Surely, our responsibility to educate our children must come before all dispensable luxuries. When expensive equipment requirements are put on us we should cut out more luxuries in our private lives as well as within our school expenditures.

There are other circumstances, no doubt, which enter into our decision regarding the establishment of a Christian school. The conclusion which we can draw from these which have been mentioned, however, is that wherever possible the

Christian community is responsible to maintain a Christian school.

Summary

The preceding discussion embraces the topic that one purpose of the Christian school is that "the world might see the willingness of teacher, parent, church, and pupil to deny Satan and self and take up Christ's cross in everything." We started with a presentation of the necessary opposition between the world and the believer noting that the believer is hated "without cause" (or at least, the obedience of the believer is hated "without cause"). We saw that one aspect and responsibility of our covenantal obedience is to train and discipline our children in covenantal obedience. Thus, Christian education is necessarily involved in covenantal obedience.

If we maintain a truly consistent Christian school, it establishes a strong witness concerning both our obedience and our concept of obedience. This witness is displayed before the "world," the "worldly," other Christians, and our own children. So, our main proposition states a truth about our Christian witness, and much incentive is to be gained from the witness which a Christian school displays before the world. Even more incentive, however, is added when the full scope of our witness is seen. The intensity and specific expressions of this witness by teacher, parent, church, and child were briefly presented. Even that brief discussion should be sufficient to establish the clarity and influence of the witness extended through a truly Christian school. Finally, we addressed the degree to which such a salutary witness should be pursued. We concluded that a Christian school is not an overpriced and unaffordable luxury, but that it meets a deep need and is a highly desirable enterprise.

Chapter 5
GOD

The Purpose of a Christian School is . . .

That Mankind Might Do Everything to God's Glory
CORNELIUS VAN TIL*

The purpose of a Christian school which underlies and directs all other purposes is to teach, to inculcate into the hearts and minds of its pupils that "Man's chief end is to glorify God and enjoy Him forever" (Westminster Shorter Catechism, Question 1).

The pupils of a Christain school must be wooed and won to know with all their minds and to love with all their hearts the Christ of the Scriptures as their Redeemer. In so doing they are also to imitate him who "executeth the offices of a Prophet, of a Priest, and of a King, both in his estate of humiliation and exaltation" (WSC, Q. 23).

The work of a man as a prophet is to set forth the meaning of the revelation of God to mankind. The work of man as a king is to govern and subdue all things so as to make them

---

*Dr. Cornelius Van Til is Professor of Apologetics, emeritus, at Westminster Seminary. For decades he has been a proponent of Christian education, and a popular speaker at Christian school conventions. His many published works include *The Defense of the Faith, The Christian Theory of Knowledge,* and *Essays on Christian Education.*

subservient to God. The work of man as a priest is to dedicate himself and all things about him to God. We were created to be prophets, priests and kings reflecting the character of our God (Eph. 4:24; Col. 3:10). It is as the Christian parent, teacher, and pupil live as true prophets, priests and kings that they reflect the character of God, and bring him honor instead of shame. However, man, through his fall into sin in Adam, has become a prophet without a mantle, a king without a crown, and a priest without a sacrifice. Fallen man is separated from God by his sin. He knows very well that he is an image-bearer of God, but he suppresses this in-created knowledge of God. He hates God and his fellow man. He is dead in breaking God's laws. He sins against his knowledge of God and his law. In his quest to suppress this in-created knowledge of God, he has usurped the place of God by assuming his own autonomous self-sufficiency.

As a result man has become a false prophet, a usurping king, and a self-serving priest. As a false prophet, man stands off from God. He seeks by his own methods to direct every effort to understand himself and the world about him. He does not use God's revelation as the final point of reference.

As a usurping king, fallen man directs all his governing activity toward himself. He does not govern with God's revelation as the final point of reference or according to the pattern of stewardship revealed to him in the Bible.

As a self-serving priest, he directs all his worship toward himself instead of toward God.

In short, fallen man has broken the covenant God made with him in Adam, and breaks the covenant over and over again in all that he does as a thinker (prophet), as an actor (king), and as a lover (priest). As such he is and abides forever under the wrath of God. In Adam all mankind was driven forth from the presence of God and will be forever separate from him. Jesus speaks of the place where the "worm dies not and the fire is not quenched" (Mark 9:48).

But now I must speak more particularly of Christian education. As the name implies, a Christian education is a

116

Christ-centered education. What must we, as teachers in a Christian school, tell our pupils about the person and work of Christ? As Christian parents, what do we tell our children? We must tell them that Christ and his work are what he himself tells us they are. We gain this information about the person and work of Christ in the Scriptures of the Old and New Testaments. A Christian education is, therefore, a Bible-centered education.

In the Scriptures, Christ tells us how he fulfills and restores the offices of prophet, priest, and king. How does Christ fulfill the office of a prophet? He does so, "in revealing to us, by His Word and Spirit, the will of God for our salvation" (WSC, Q. 24). In other words, he proclaims to us the *truth* pertaining to God, the world, and our deliverance from the consequences of our rebellion over against the *lie* of Satan.

When Adam believed Satan instead of God, he made a league with hell. He became a partner with Satan in his effort to hold under, to repress in unrighteousness, the truth as it is in Jesus. But Christ undoes this damage by fulfilling the office of prophet. He reveals how the Father may be known. He bears witness to the truth of God's Word, and he commands all men to be reconciled to God. He opens up the way for us to be true prophets of God once again by revealing to us what we are to believe concerning God, his law, and the world he has placed us in. Looking at the world through the "spectacles" of God's Word, we are able to understand the world and our place in it from God's perspective. We are no longer prophets without a mantle, for Jesus commissions us to "go into all the world and preach the Gospel."

How does Christ fulfill the office of a priest? He fulfills that office, "in His once offering up Himself a sacrifice to satisfy divine justice, and reconcile us to God" (WSC, Q. 25). As a prophet, Christ pronounces divine judgement upon us. We have rejected God's rule over us. The sentence for spiritual treason is death. But in fulfilling the office of a priest Jesus mediates to us divine mercy. Specifically he offered himself through his suffering and death on the cross as a sacrifice to satisfy divine justice and reconcile us to God, being at the same time the sacrifice and the priest who offered it (Eph. 4:1-10).

In being our priest Jesus has freed us to be true priests once again. We no longer serve ourselves, but him who loved us. While we do not need to make sacrifices for our sin, we are free to make sacrifices of thanksgiving.

How does Christ fulfill the office of a king? "In subduing us to himself, in ruling and defending us, and in restraining and conquering all his and our enemies" (WSC, Q. 26). As a teacher in a Christian school, I must tell my pupils about the struggle between God and the devil for the possession of men. I must tell them about this holy war. I must tell them that this war is global in nature and universal in extent. The devil denies that "the earth is the Lord's and all it contains," and he seeks to convince others of his error. There is nothing on earth or in heaven which the devil has not pre-empted for himself.

He would have men forget that they are image-bearers of God created to glorify and enjoy God forever and are subject to him. Instead he would have men believe that they are alone in a universe without God and a world without meaning. In the process he would lead them to reject God's view of the world as revealed in the Scriptures, and substitute one of their own making. In short, the devil desires men to follow the way that seems right to them, to let them decide for themselves what they would believe, without letting on that such a way of life is the way of death. This is the spiritual warfare that rages all around us.

But Jesus Christ came into the world to establish his kingdom (i.e., the kingdom of God and of Heaven) upon the ruins of the kingdom of Satan. As the way, the truth, and the life, Christ destroyed the devil as the false way (error), as false truth (the lie), and as false life (death).

To bring out these truths as a Christian parent and teacher, I must follow the course of the development of the kingdom of Christ throughout the course of history. I must talk to my children about (1) Christ and Adam, (2) Christ and Noah, (3) Christ and Abraham, (4) Christ and Moses, and (5) Christ and Paul.

Christ and Adam

God told Adam that he must develop the resources of creation to the praise of his Maker. He must develop himself as a self-conscious prophet, priest, and king to God. God has made man to be and to become a covenant keeper. God told Adam, and in Adam as their representative he told all men, to become increasingly conscious of their relationship to God. Man was to exercise dominion over the earth. Man was to freely enjoy all that the earth had to provide, but only as vice-regent, under and in submission to the Lord, the Creator of heaven and earth. Throughout their generations men were to tell their children that such was their task. They would find great joy as they carried forth this, their cultural obligation to have dominion over and subdue the earth under God. Their reward would be eternal life. But, if they disobeyed, they would die. They would be cast out of the presence of God forever and ever.

Satan was aware of this covenant, this arrangement that God made with man. Using the serpent as his instrument, he deceived Eve and Eve drew Adam into disobedience against the love-law of God their Creator.

"Be yourself," Satan had said in effect to Adam. "God does not control whatever comes to pass. God is not higher than we are. Do not let him tell you what is true and what is not true. Be your own standard in all that you say or think. God is not the Creator and sustainer of this world as you think. We and God are just fellow creatures on this earth that just "happens" to be here. God cannot possibly punish you if you "disobey" him; he, as well as we, is but a floating leaf on a shoreless, bottomless ocean of chance. As he controls nothing more than we do, so he knows nothing more than

119

we. How could he conceivably call you to account for your behavior?"

All this sounded beautiful, *very* beautiful to Adam and to Eve. Now they were on their own. Now they could have real communion with one another. No longer would God peek through their living room, their bedroom, and their kitchen. "Glory to us in the highest! But let us not be selfish. Let us invite God to join us so that, together with us, he may explore himself and the things about us. God is much older than we are. No doubt he can teach us from his long experience what is true and what is false, what is right and what is wrong, what is beautiful and what is ugly. And surely we can help him in return. With the dew of youth upon us we can help him overcome the rigidity of his way of life. God is what he is *for us* and we are what we are *for him*. Thus God and we shall have a common history. Together we shall enlarge our borders and strengthen our stakes. Man's chief end is to glorify God and enjoy him forever and God's chief end is to glorify man and enjoy him forever."

"There is a way that seemeth good unto a man, but the end thereof are the ways of death" (Prov. 16:25). Adam and Eve heeded the evil advice of Satan. Rejecting the truth, they ate of the tree, embracing a lie, with fearsome results: "Our first parents, being left to the freedom of their own will, fell from the estate wherein they were created, by sinning against God" (WSC, Q. 13). "The covenant being made with Adam, not only for himself, but for his posterity, all mankind descending from him by ordinary generation, sinned in him, and fell with him in his first transgression" (WSC, Q. 16). "All mankind, by their fall, lost communion with God, are under his wrath and curse, and so made liable to all the miseries in this life, to death itself, and to the pains of hell forever" (WSC, Q. 19).

But God did not leave all mankind to perish in the estate of sin and misery, "for God having out of his mere good pleasure and from all eternity elected some to everlasting life, did enter into a covenant of grace to deliver them out of the

120

estate of sin and misery, and to bring them into an estate of salvation by a Redeemer" (WSC, Q. 20). God revealed his plan in his promise to Satan: "I will put enmity between you and the woman, and between your seed and her seed, he shall bruise your head, and you shall bruise his heel" (Gen. 3:15). As a parent and as a Christian school teacher I must make clear from the beginning this basic reason why man does not glorify God, yet at the same time relate our hope in Christ who bruised the serpent's head.

Christ and Noah

As a teacher in a Christian school, I would then proceed to point out how this promise unfolded in the history of God's revelation. However, during the period from Adam to Noah, Satan seemed to be bruising the head of the seed of the woman: "Then the Lord saw that the wickedness of man was great on earth, and that every intent of the thoughts of his heart was only evil continually. And the Lord was sorry that He had made man on earth, and He was grieved in His heart. And the Lord said, 'I will blot out man whom I have created from the face of the land, from man to animals to creeping things and to birds of the sky; for I am sorry that I have made them.' But Noah found favor in the eyes of the Lord" (Gen. 6:5-8).

Noah was not one man in a million, but one man among all mankind. Christ, the promised Redeemer, speaks to and works through this one man, Noah. Saved by grace alone he became a "preacher of righteousness," the only covenant-keeper as over against all other men as covenant-breakers. God appears to Noah and tells him to warn his contemporaries of the coming flood. "And behold, I, even I am bringing the flood of water upon the earth, to destroy all flesh in which is the breath of life, from under heaven; everything that is on the earth shall perish. But I will establish My covenant with you; and you shall enter the ark–you and your sons and your wife, and your sons' wives with you. And of

121

every living thing or all flesh, you shall bring two of every kind into the ark, to keep them alive with you; they shall be male and female" (Gen. 6:17-19). "Thus Noah did; according to all that God has commanded him, so he did" (Gen. 6:22).

By being obedient, Noah was doing what Adam and Eve failed to do. He was ordering his life according to the revealed will of God. Yet he was surely challenged by those in his day who believed the lie of Satan, and had rejected the presence and rule of God in the world. Certainly it would appear foolish to them for a man to build a huge boat on dry land.

Noah, however, proceeded at once to the building of the ark. After some decades, the ark began to take on something of the appearance it would eventually have. His carpenters were well pleased with their employer. He paid them high wages; no strikes for them! "But, Mr. Noah," they questioned, "How can you expect to float this ark when it is ready? We're here on top of the highest mountain." Fathers and mothers took their children to see this strange sight and this peculiar man. They snickered. During the last day, they laughed him to scorn.

One of them said, "Mr. Noah, surely you are with us in following the empirical method, the method of scientific observation. There are records of high floods, but not of such a flood as you tell us will come upon us. You tell us you are building your ark on the authority of God, the God who first spoke to Adam and threatened him with death if he should eat the 'forbidden fruit'! Do you really think that this story of Adam's disobedience and fall is anything more than a myth?"

Noah simply kept on witnessing to the men of his day of the coming judgment for their disobedience in Adam. On the authority of the Lord speaking to him, Noah told these people that spoke with him that soon they would all die in the all-covering flood and that the rains would descend and the fountains of the deep would open up, both of them in unison. As servants of the Lord he and his family would be safe in the ark sharing in the victory of the Redeemer of mankind who was bruising the head of the serpent.

It is Noah's willingness to hold fast to God's perspective on the world that illustrates the purpose of a Christian school. From his submission to the reality of God's power and his acceptance of the authority of God's Word, we receive insight into the nature of Christian education. Our way of life, like Noah's, must begin on the Word of God as over against all human authorities and experts. Like Noah, we must instill in ourselves and in our children the desire to become "preachers of righteousness." On the authority of God's Word we must instruct our students about the meaning of life, and character of the world, and even the limitations of science. Our loyalty to the Word of God and our love for the Savior of whom it speaks should affect every aspect of our lives (II Pet. 3:1-7).

Christ and Abraham

When the Lord speaks with Abraham he takes a second step forward. God now reveals how he is going to fulfill the promise to bruise the head of the serpent. He is going to establish a nation through which he will carry out his redemptive purposes. "Go forth from your country, and from your relatives and from your father's house, to the land that I will show you; and I will make you a great nation, and I will bless you, and make your name great; and so you shall be a blessing; and I will bless those who bless you, and the one who curses you I will curse. And in you all the families of the earth shall be blessed" (Gen 12:1-3).

In order to establish this nation, God makes a covenant with Abraham to give him numberless decendants and the land of Palestine which he lived in as a foreigner: " 'As for me, behold, my covenant is with you, and you shall be the father of a multitude of nations. No longer shall your name be called Abram, but your name shall be Abraham; for I will

123

make you the father of a multitude of nations. And I will make you exceedingly fruitful, and I will make nations of you, and kings shall come forth from you. And I will establish my covenant between me and you and your descendants after you throughout their generations for an everlasting covenant, to be God to you and to your descendants after you. And I will give to you and to your decendants after you, the land of your sojournings, all the land of Canaan, for an everlasting possession; and I will be their God.' God said further to Abraham, 'Now as for you, you shall keep my covenant, you and your descendants after you throughout their generations. This is my covenant, which you shall keep between me and you and your descendants after you: every male among you shall be circumcised.' " "Then Abraham took Ishmael his son, and all the servants who were born in his house and all who were bought with his money, every male among the men of Abraham's household, and circumcised the flesh of their foreskin in the very same day, as God had said to him" (Gen. 17: 4-10, 23).

Having read these words to my pupils, I would point out to them that the Redeemer of mankind is making definite progress in his work of bruising the head of the serpent. God's covenant with Abraham is a pivotal point in Bible history. All the rest of Scripture explains how God fulfilled these promises to Abraham.

At the same time, Abraham is called the "Father of the faithful." Why? Because "Abraham believed in the Lord and he reckoned it to him as righteousness" (Gen. 15:6). Because of this Abraham's faith is a model to all the faithful. He is a living example of what it means to be a covenant-keeper. The goals of his life suggest to us what the goals of Christian or covenant education should be.

How is Abraham a model for Christian education? First, he is a model in his obedience of faith: "By faith Abraham, when he was called, obeyed by going out to a place which he was to receive for an inheritance; and he went out, not knowing where he was going" (Heb. 11:8). Abraham trusted the

124

Word of God. He trusted God and moved to Canaan even though the wisdom of the age would have branded him a fool. He trusted God and believed that he would provide him a son despite the medical opinion of his day. Abraham believed God's Word, and so must we if we would be true sons of Abraham and heirs according to the promises given to him.

Second, Abraham is a model in his patience of faith: "By faith he lived as an alien in the land of promise, as in a foreign land, dwelling in tents with Isaac and Jacob, fellow-heirs of the same promise" (Heb. 11:9). Abraham never owned any of the land promised to him except a small part which he purchased as a grave site for Sarah, yet he trusted the Lord to deliver what he promised. God did deliver. He made of Abraham a great nation through which the promised seed of the woman did come to bruise the head of the serpent.

Finally, Abraham was a model in his hope of faith: "for he was looking for the city which has foundations, whose architect and builder is God" (Heb. 11:10). Abraham's faith looked ahead to the time when God would accomplish all that he had promised. He had a set hope in the promises because he had a sure hope in God. We must have that same endurance of faith, for, "... in the last days mockers will come with their mocking, following after their own lusts, and saying, 'Where is the promise of His coming?' For ever since the fathers fell asleep, all continues just as it was from the beginning of creation.... But do not let this one fact escape your notice, beloved, that with the Lord one day is a thousand years, and a thousand years as one day. The Lord is not slow about His promise, as some count slowness, but is patient toward you, not wishing for any to perish, but for all to come to repentance. But the day of the Lord will come like a thief, in which the heavens will pass away with a roar and the elements will be destroyed with intense heat, and the earth and its works will be burned up. Since all these things are to be destroyed in this way, what sort of people ought you to be in holy conduct and godliness, looking for and hastening the coming of the day of God, . . . but according to his promise we are looking for new heavens and a new earth, in which righteousness dwells" (II Peter 3:3, 4, 8-13).

Christ and Moses

By means of the character and work of Moses, the Redeemer of mankind made another large step forward in his work of bruising the head of the serpent.

Moses was the mediator of the old covenant. In that role he typified the office of prophet, priest, and king which found their ultimate fulfillment in the mediator of the new covenant, the Lord Jesus. Nevertheless, the example of Moses is instructive to us and our students of what it means to be a covenant-keeper.

Moses was the "meekest" of all men. This does not mean the he was a Casper Milquetoast, but that he trusted the Lord to preserve, protect, and defend him. Moses recognized that his strength was not in himself, but in the Lord, and because he humbled himself, God highly exalted him. He is Moses, the man of God. He is the prophet, priest and king of the old covenant.

Moses was the great prophet of the old covenant. "Since then, no prophet has risen in Israel like Moses whom the Lord knew face to face" (Num. 34:10). As the great prophet of the old covenant, Moses gave the covenant people the law of God, the ordinances of Jehovah God. By this law Moses was to organize a nation, a nation of Abrahams. Through this nation and the revelation which God gave to it, all the nations of the world would be blessed.

Through Moses, the great king of the old covenant, the Lord led his people dry shod through the Red Sea, while the hosts of Pharaoh drowned, every one of them. Through Moses his servant, the Redeemer of mankind led his people through the desert wilds, where no man dwelt and where no water was, toward the promised land. As king, Moses also organized the people of Israel so that the armies of the Lord could destroy Amalek.

As the great priest of the old covenant, Moses offered sacrifices and prayers on behalf of the people of God. He directed the observance of the Passover through which the people of Israel were delivered from the angel of death and freed from the land of Egypt, the house of bondage. He also interceded for the covenant people with the Lord, lest God should destroy them for their idol worship, or send them into the land without his presence.

As a true servant of the Lord, Moses is an example of what it means to be a covenant keeper and a Christian school teacher. In following his example as a prophet, we should teach diligently the Word of God to the children entrusted to our care. In following his example as king, we must warn them about the enemies of God, and equip them against the onslaughts of false teaching and other stumbling blocks to faith. In following his example as priest, we must point our young people to the one true passover and sacrifice for sin— the death of the Lord Jesus Christ as the only way which they can be released from their bondage to sin and Satan.

Christ and Paul

This brings us to the last and greatest step forward in God's work of redemption--the coming of the Redeemer himself. Christ, as the mediator of the new covenant, is the one who bruises the head of the serpent.

As the writer of Hebrews says, "Therefore, holy brethren, partakers of a heavenly calling, consider Jesus, the Apostle and High Priest of our confession. He was faithful to him who appointed him, as Moses also was in all his house. For he has been counted worthy of more glory than Moses, but just so much as the builder of the house has more honor than the house. . . . Now Moses was faithful in all his house as a servant, for a testimony of those things which were to be spoken later; but Christ was faithful as a Son over his house, whose house we are, if we hold fast our confidence and the boast of our hope firm until the end" (Heb. 3:1-6).

As members of the household of God, and as those who seek to be good stewards of it in our task as Christian school teachers and Christian parents, there is a ministry of encouragement entrusted to us. As the writer of Hebrews goes on to say, "Take care, brethren, lest there should be in any one of you an evil, unbelieving heart, in falling away from the living God. But encourage one another day after day, as long as it is still called 'Today,' lest any one of you be hardened by the deceitfulness of sin. For we have become partakers of Christ, if we hold fast the beginning of our assurance firm until the end" (Heb. 3:12-13).

The need of such encouragement is real, for the forces of unbelief are all around us. No one understands this better than the apostle Paul. Speaking on behalf of the Great Physician, Paul diagnoses the case of fallen man. Paul finds man to be suffering from a sickness unto death. He tells us that this sickness consists of rebellion against God, and that, therefore, "the wrath of God is revealed from heaven against all ungodliness and unrighteousness of men, who suppress the truth in unrighteousness, because that which is known about God is evident within them; for God made it evident to them. For since the creation of the world his invisible attributes, his eternal power and divine nature, have been clearly seen, being understood through what has been made, so that they are without excuse. For even though they knew God, they did not honor him as God, or give thanks; but they became futile in their speculations, and their foolish heart was darkened. Professing to be wise, they became fools, and exchanged the glory of the incorruptible God for an image of the form of corruptible man and of birds and four-footed animals and crawling creatures" (Rom. 1:18-23).

To this mass of corruption Paul brings the gospel of Christ and him crucified, of Christ and his resurrection. "For I delivered to you," says Paul, "as of first importance what I also received, that Christ died for our sins according to the Scriptures, and that He was buried, and He was raised on the third day according to the Scriptures" (I Cor. 15:3, 4). "Therefore, just as through one man sin entered into the world, and death through sin, and so death spread to all men, because all sinned. . . . But the free gift is not like the transfression. For if by the transgression of the one the many died, much more did the grace of God and the gift by the grace of the one Man, Jesus Christ, abound to the many. . . . For if by the transgression of the one, death reigned through the one, much more those who receive the abundance of grace and of the gift of righteousness will reign in life through the One, Jesus Christ" (Rom. 5:12, 15, 17). "But I am not ashamed of the gospel, for it is the power of God for salvation to every one who believes, . . . for in it the righteousness of God is revealed from faith to faith; as it is written, 'But he who is righteous by faith shall live' " (Rom 1:16, 17 marg, NASB).

It is through this salvation by grace provided by the death and resurrection of our Lord that we can hold fast the confidence of our faith firm to the end. It is the truth of the gospel which enables us to declare with authority that the earth belongs to the Lord, and through Him, to us. Says Paul, "What shall we say to these things? If God is for us, who is against us? He who did not spare his own Son, but delivered him up for us all, how will he not also with him freely give us all things? Who will bring a charge against God's elect? God is the one who justifies; who is the one who condemns? Christ Jesus is he who died, Yes, rather who was raised, who is at the right hand of God, who also intercedes for us. Who shall separate us from the love of Christ? Shall tribulation, or distress, or persecution, or famine, or nakedness, or peril of sword?. . .in all these things we overwhelmingly conquer through Him who loved us. For I am convinced that neither death, nor life, nor angels, nor principalities, nor things present, nor things to come, nor powers, nor height, nor depth, nor any other created thing, shall be able to separate us from the love of God, which is in Christ Jesus our Lord"

(Rom. 8:31-39). As Paul summarizes elsewhere, "all things belong to you, and you belong to Christ, and Christ belongs to God" (I Cor. 3:22).

So then, as a parent I tell my own children, and as a teacher I tell my students what Christ says to me through Adam, through Noah, through Abraham, through Moses, and through Paul. If by the regenerating electing grace of God we have died with Christ to our sins and risen with him unto righteousness, then we shall seek to subdue all things unto him and God shall be all and in all. Having put on the whole armor of God, we shall destroy speculation and every lofty thing raised up against the knowledge of God. As covenant keepers, we will make every thought captive to the obedience of Christ.

If we do this we shall once again be true prophets as we declare the significance of God's revelation in the Bible. We will once again be true kings as we seek to make all things subject to the service of God. We shall once again be true priests as we offer up our bodies as living sacrifices acceptable to God, seeking to do everything to his glory.

To bring to all men everywhere the message of salvation, and to bring all of creation in subjection to the Creator—this is our cultural, our redemptive mandate. And this is the purpose of a Christian school.

The Purpose, Basis, and Declaration of the Christian Education Association

PURPOSE

Because the Sovereign Triune God calls men everywhere to think His thoughts after Him, to exercise dominion over all things according to His will, and to consecrate themselves and all things unto Him, we are bound to obey this divine command. Therefore, since education today is largely controlled by anti-Christian philosophies, we, in pursuit of the divine mandate, establish a Christian Education Association. The purpose of this association is to assist Christian educators and concerned parents in the task of teaching their children through the collection, publication, and distribution of literature produced by competent Christian writers. The contributions of these writers will assist in understanding the true basis for knowledge, and the proper integration of that knowledge, in the various fields of learning.

BASIS

The supreme standard of the Association shall be the Scriptures of the Old and New Testaments as the Word of God, the only infallible rule of faith and practice.

The Association also adopts as standards, subordinate to the Word of God, the Belgic Confession, the Heidelberg Catechism, and the Canons of Dort approved or formulated by the Synod of Dort, and the Confession of Faith, the Larger Catechism and the Shorter Catechism formulated by the Westminster Assembly, as setting forth the system of truth taught in the Holy Scriptures.

For those not acquainted with these standards, they affirm primarily:

1. That God, the Creator of the world, is wholly in control of it, working out His purposes for His own glory.
2. That the authority of the Scriptures rests totally on God and that this authority is true in every area of life.
3. That man, created innocent, sinned and thus utterly forfeited his communion with God, so that apart from God's grace he remains totally lost in every area of life.
4. That Jesus Christ, truly God and truly man, accomplished salvation for His people through the shedding of blood by His death on the cross, this work of grace being confirmed by God's raising Him from the dead.
5. That the salvation offered through Jesus is not realized by any effort of man, but only by the ministry of the Holy Spirit who alone brings man to repentance and faith, imparts spiritual life, and applies the Word of God to believers both individually and corporately in the Church.

DECLARATION

In accordance with the position set forth in the BASIS and in pursuit of the design set forth in the PURPOSE, the Association declares as follows:

Recognizing God as the Creator, Sustainer, and Redeemer of the Universe in Jesus Christ, we confess that He alone understands fully the nature and purposes of His creation. Therefore, we can have true knowledge about ourselves and our world only when we pattern our understanding of this world after God's understanding of it as revealed to us in the Scriptures. It follows that, even though in virture of man's being created in the image of God and the non-saving operations of the Holy Spirit men receive knowledge, in a certain sense, apart from the illumination derived from the Scriptures, yet in any department of reality knowledge is true in the fullest sense only if it is illumined by, and is faithful to, the Holy Scriptures, the inspired Word of truth.

As a corollary to this, we repudiate and expose as anti-Christian any scientific methodology or philosophic position which would cause men to question or deny the self-sufficient and self-existent Triune God, His written revelation of Himself, or any aspect of the world as He has interpreted it for us in that revelation.

An Association which has as its objective the promotion of the knowledge of the truth and the glory of God must insure that the principles that underlie and guide its studies in every area of learning shall be derived from the Scriptures. Therefore each study published and promoted by this Association shall rest upon and present its case in accordance with presuppositions of the Christian faith, and shall subject its whole procedure as well as its conclusions to the scrutiny and direction of the full and complete revelation of God in the Scriptures of the Old and New Testaments.

For further information about the Christian Education Association, please address all inquiries to Christian Education Association, 6931 Highland, Hanover Park, Illinois, 60103.

Related titles prepared for publication include:
The Basis for a Christian School: A Resource Book with Answers for the Christian Parent, with chapters by Joseph Bayly, Charles Schauffle, David Cummings, John Whitehead, and Mark Noll.
How to Have a Quality Christian School: A Practical Guide to Quality with Questions for Faculty and Classroom Discussion, by Norman DeJong.